Speaker, Missionary and Co-Founder of *Global Impact Group, Inc.* If you have ever felt stuck in a season of life, or overwhelmed by the challenges life has brought, this book is for you! Kathy pours out real wisdom and insightful encouragement for walking fearlessly in *Unexpected Seasons*. I love how she walks us through personal experiences mixed with biblical direction as she teaches us to rest, trust in God, find the courage to fight well, and thrive in each season of life. I'll be going back to this book often!

– Elana Wilkins
Speaker and Lead Pastor of *CityLife Church*, San Francisco, California

My friend Kathy Cannistraci has a unique, non-pretentious, down to earth relatable perspective on the various seasons of life. Her book provides today's women with an abundance of incredible, real-life practical experiences, combined with a wealth of reassuring biblical insight on how to weather life's seasonal storms both expected and unexpected. Kathy speaks from experience in her life, family and from years of caring for the women of the church and community. This must-read is a treasure you will want in your library.

– Marilyn Kiteley
Pastor Emeritus, *Shiloh Church*, Oakland, California

Kathy Cannistraci has been an inspiration to so many women, including myself. I have known Kathy since we were kids and have always admired how she has lived her life with grace and strength whether a young pregnant mom moving to the Philippines or a grandmother pastoring alongside her husband in a thriving church in California. I have watched her walk through each season of her life with strong faith in God and trust in His ability to take care of her. *Unexpected Seasons* will help thousands of women around the world to walk through whatever season they are in and find God's grace and strength to help them in their time of need.

– LaNell C. Miller
Speaker, International missionary, Author and blogger of *MoreThanJustABoob.com*, Co-Pastor of *Church on the Rock*, Texarkana, Texas

I have known Kathy since she was a teenager and have always loved her authenticity, it shines through in this book. We can't control our circumstances, but we can control how we respond to them. I deeply appreciate Kathy's approach. She uses practical life and Scriptural examples to masterfully equip us for the seasons of life and helps us to make the most of them. Every woman, young or old will greatly benefit from reading *Unexpected Seasons*.

– Priscilla Johnson
Speaker, Missionary, and Co-Pastor of *Reset Church*, Berlin, Germany

WHAT LEADERS ARE SAYING...

Change is here to stay! Pastor Kathy Cannistraci emphasizes that truth in her book, *Unexpected Seasons*. She helps the reader recognize the leading of the Lord as the person navigates through the many changes in life.

God has the power to turn your current season from a time of confusion, sorrow, or grief into a season of recovery. You will experience fresh hope for your future as you read this book. I recommend *Unexpected Seasons* for anyone desiring to move through life's difficult places and discover God's full purpose for their life!

– Barbara Wentroble
President, *International Breakthrough Ministries*
President, *Breakthrough Business Leaders*
Speaker and Author of 11 books including *Council Room of the Lord, Access the Power of God, Access Your Prophetic Gift, Prophetic Intercession, Empowered for Your Purpose,* and *Fighting for Your Prophetic Promise*

Unexpected Seasons is a must-read for every woman who wants God's best for her life. Kathy's sincerity and authenticity will inspire you to step into every season of life with courage and confidence. The Biblical foundation of the book will give every reader the essentials for success in life through every circumstance. It will inspire you to grow and empower others to find their God-given purpose by coming to know Christ as their personal Saviour and experiencing His love through every season of life.

– Heather Mullen
Co-Founder, *Home Church Canada*
Host, *'One in a Million'* Women's Conference

Kathy Cannistraci is the ideal person to write *Unexpected Seasons*. She has overcome, learned, and grown in the seasons of her life. A long time Pastor, she has also observed, helped, and encouraged scores of women of all ages to grow and flourish in their seasons. Kathy has beautifully woven her experience in life's journeys with her gift of teaching to create an inspirational treasure. You will understand she has lived what she is sharing. As a friend and colleague, Kathy has supported me in some of my seasons. You will love this book, whatever season you are in!"

– Mary Alice Islieb
Executive Director, *Christian Outreach International*
Speaker and Author of *Effective Fervent Prayer* and *Healing Toxic Emotions*

Kathy Cannistraci invites you to learn from her personal journey as a seasoned woman and a gifted leader. Her book *Unexpected Seasons* will both encourage and challenge you with helpful insights on navigating life's passages and transitions with grace, unshakeable faith and a firm conviction that God has not forgotten you. As Kathy shares Biblical principles and real-life stories, allow yourself to not only embrace the season you are in but to dream again about tomorrow.

– Sharon Damazio
Pastor, Speaker and Musical artist of 22 songs including, *In Christ Alone*.

Kathy Cannistraci is an authentic woman of God who is genuine and transparent. She offers wisdom laced with grace. Her book will stir hope within you during the most demanding seasons of life and bring fresh understanding that even in a rainfall, God will still produce a precious harvest, a humble heart, and incredible rewards.

– China Cleveland

ACKNOWLEDGEMENTS

Heartfelt thanks to the women and men who have inspired me to write *Unexpected Seasons* and played a major part in this book by allowing me to share their inspirational life stories.

Cari Stewart, my friend, and co-worker in Christ, graciously shared her Winter Season with us.

Carol Avila, my sister, who prayed me into the Kingdom of God, shared her Summer Season with us.

Joanne Sullivan, my sister, who bought me my first Bible and shared parts of her Summer Season with us.

My husband, David Cannistraci, for inspiring me in my walk with the Lord day after day and for challenging me to do more for Jesus every day.

My sons, who are serving the Lord and love God with all their hearts.

My editors, Karen Greenwell and Sharon Gregory who spent countless hours reading, editing and sharing their own life-changing stories from their books:

Romance with the Master by Karen Greenwell

From Tragedy to Triumph by Sharon Gregory

Carrie Cannistraci, Photographic Design

Jordan Cannistraci, Cover Design

Unexpected Seasons

Kathy Cannistraci

© Copyright 2018 Kathy Cannistraci

All rights reserved. No part of this book may be reproduced or transmitted in any form or by any means, electronic or mechanical, including photocopying and recording, or by any information storage and retrieval system, except in the case of brief quotations for use in articles, reviews, without written permission from the author.

The views expressed in this book are the author's and do not necessarily reflect those of the publisher.

7710-T Cherry Park Dr, Ste 224

Houston, TX 77095

http://WorldwidePublishingGroup.com
(713) 766-4271

ISBN: 978-1684116263

CONTENTS

ACKNOWLEDGMENTS .... **v**

FOREWORD .... **xi**

INTRODUCTION .... **xv**

1 UNDERSTANDING NATURAL AND SPIRITUAL SEASONS 1

Understanding God's pattern for natural seasons gives insight into your spiritual seasons. With every passing season, God gives more understanding of His wonderful purpose for your life.

2 IT'S COLD OUTSIDE **13**

So many women have walked through a cold, personal Winter season—possibly with a loss of a loved one, a divorce, or loss of a job or a business. You can't control your season, but you can choose to believe God's promises during a Winter season.

3 IT'S SPRINGTIME **27**

You will discover Spring is not only a time for enjoying life, but it is a time for you to invest and move forward to assure your future harvest. It's a time of anticipating good things.

4 SUMMER AND THE KINGDOM OF GOD **53**

When you're experiencing a Summer season you may be enjoying the benefits of the seeds of love that were planted in your Spring season. You can learn the secret of growing in your relationship with God in the

Summer and will see dramatic changes take place in your heart as you believe what God says about you in His Word.

5 THE COLORS ARE ABOUT TO CHANGE 89

God will use changing seasons to show you He has a purpose for every event in your life. He will challenge you to do things you never thought you could do. He will take you to places that you couldn't possibly go in your own strength.

6 A TIME FOR FULFILLMENT 101

Get ready for a season of rewards for being a good and faithful steward over the things God has entrusted to you. Jesus commended the trustworthy servants in Matthew 25:23 for being loyal over the small responsibilities He gave them and He rewarded them for their faithfulness.

7 THIS IS YOUR BEST SEASON 119

God leads you through the dark nights of the soul, inspires you to get back on your feet and helps you to move forward into the greatest season you've ever known. He's calling you to reach up into heavenly places and live in the abundant life He's planned for you.

FOREWORD
J. Lee Grady

Back in 2017, I was in a church in Idaho listening to my daughter, Margaret, preach a sermon from Psalm 45 about fighting injustice. As she shared passionately about why she adopted an African child and how she traveled to India to fight gender-based violence, I wept—not because my daughter was preaching, but because I could hear God's voice thundering out of the heart of a 31-year-old mother who cares about the poor and the mistreated.

Sometimes it takes a woman to reflect God's heart.

I've been a vocal advocate for women in ministry since my book *10 Lies the Church Tells Women* was published in 2000. I have helped many pastors remove the traditional barriers to women, and I've encouraged countless women to fully embrace God's unique calling—even when this requires scary steps of faith into uncharted territory.

But I have found that many women struggle to find their place in the body of Christ, either because of traditionalism and gender bias in the church or because they don't understand their unique spiritual gifts or the spiritual season they are in at the moment.

It was not long after my first book was published that I met Kathy Cannistraci and her husband, David, at their church in California. When I met Kathy, I could tell she is a woman who is comfortable in her own skin. She came to the realization years ago that she does not have to conform to other people's expectations. She is just Kathy. She does not wear a "pastor's wife" mask, nor does she have to pretend to have gifts she doesn't. She doesn't have to fulfill a list of duties that religious culture places on her.

She is free to be the woman God called her to be.

And that is why I am so thrilled she has written this book to help women discover their identity in Christ. Kathy knows that a woman's identity is not just about "who" she really is but "when" she is. She understands the seasons of a woman's life.

It really annoys me when Christians force people to fit into neat categories. For years we've done this with gender. I wish I had a dollar for every time a preacher has claimed that "all men hide their feelings," or "all women are domestic," or "all men refuse to ask for directions."

Those are stereotypes. While God made only two genders, men and women come in all types. Our uniqueness is shaped by our bodies, skills, interests, personality quirks, communication styles, ethnicity, life experiences and so much more.

A few years ago, Christian organizations invented questionnaires and tests to determine a person's spiritual gifts. I've taken all these tests, and sometimes they helped me understand myself better. Yet I always end up feeling like a misfit because I don't stay inside the lines. I certainly don't fit the stereotypes.

For years I've struggled to put a label on what I do in ministry. Am I a prophet? (Prophecy often flows out of me when I minister in a church setting.) Am I a teacher? (I teach regularly in ministry schools.) Am I a pastor? (I don't lead a local church, yet I mentor and disciple many young leaders.)

I recently went through an identity crisis. I was tired of people asking me, "What are you?" and my response was to blankly stare back. I wanted a label. I wanted to fit in a clear-cut category. Yet I felt like a weirdo because I don't see my odd combination of gifts and talents in most surveys.

I decided to take my own gifts assessment test by asking some friends to describe my ministry in their own words. I asked them to text me one sentence, but many of them wrote paragraphs. They often used words like "prophet," "teacher," "encourager," "apostle," "mentor" and "father's heart." But I noticed one common thread: Several guys wrote: "Your ministry is versatile. Don't worry about fitting in a box. You don't need to feel any pressure to fit a mold."

I wanted to categorize myself. But God's answer was a pleasant surprise: I don't need to fit in! Rather, I just need to stay connected to God and let Him manifest Himself through me however He wants!

Did you know that one DNA molecule in your body has enough coded information to fill 100 30-volume sets of encyclopedias? That's more than 2.25 million pages of computer code! If all the DNA in your body were joined from end to end, it would stretch 94 billion miles. And that code is different from any other person who has ever lived.

We know our fingerprints are unique from everyone else. Now, researchers have discovered that scanning the iris of the eye is five times more effective than fingerprinting because there are 240 unique features in your iris to prove it's yours! Scientists are also discovering the same uniqueness in our retinas, our faces, our insulin and the protein molecules in one strand of our hair.

King David wrote: "I will give thanks to You, for I am fearfully and wonderfully made; wonderful are Your works, and my soul knows it very well" (Psalm 139:14, NASB). If you are this unique in a biological sense, how much more is it true in the Spirit? We have been fashioned by the Creator to manifest His power in a unique way.

As you read this book, let God show you how He sees you. Let Him define you. Let Him show you your unique gifts. And let Him show you where and when you are in your journey so that you know what season of life you are in at this time. Embrace your season and enjoy the journey!

J. Lee Grady

Author, *10 Lies the Church Tells Women*
Director, The Mordecai Project

INTRODUCTION

I am on my morning walk on the two-mile path and I am looking at the beautiful Pacific Ocean on the south side of Maui, Hawaii. There are other vacationers enjoying the warm sun with their loved ones, too. It's the end of Spring and Summertime is almost here. The temperature usually stays in the low eighties during this time of year and the water looks so inviting. The ocean is as calm as a lake with barely any waves—the best time to go snorkeling. It calls my name and says, "Come in, the water's fine." I can see three-foot turtles floating on the surface of the water having their morning swim. I decided that this year I'm going to take time to enjoy the lovely sights, sounds, and fragrances of Hawaii. There are always Plumeria flowers in bloom, pineapples, and coconuts to enjoy. I'm going to capture every moment and memorize this beautiful time, so I can take it back home to California.

Every morning when my husband, David, and I wake up, we get our workout clothes on, drive across the street to one of the many beaches in the neighborhood and start our workout together. We feel truly blessed and thankful to once again be together on this beautiful island. This is how we unwind and refresh from our busy ministries as lead pastors of *GateWay City Church* in San Jose, California. We can already feel the stress melting away as we hold hands and walk towards the path. We talk about the blessings and challenges we've been through together this past year. We've been taking this walk together in Maui for twenty plus years— our home away from home.

Sometimes we reminisce about the time we met in the Winter of 1975 at an all-night prayer meeting at our church during the Christmas holiday. He admits he didn't go there to pray, but to meet the cute new girl, me. He was fourteen and I was sixteen. We were married six years later in the month of January. When I look at our wedding photos, we look like two babies, just fresh out of teenage years. He was twenty and I was twenty-two. We were both heavily involved in all our church activities. I had a full-time job in San Francisco, commuting three hours to and from work daily, while he worked at the church seven days a week during those first years of our marriage.

Eight years of marriage and two sons later, we were headed to Hawaii to visit with David's parents, a stopover on our way to be missionaries in the Philippines with our sons, ages three years and three months. We packed everything that would fit into two six-foot duffle bags to take with us on our journey. Since then we have celebrated thirty-six wedding anniversaries. Aaron and Jordan are now married with their own children. Now we're empty nesters and walking on the path that lines the Pacific Ocean in Wailea, Maui.

As the days roll on during our vacation, we get more rested and start dreaming about the future of our lives together. And of course, we always talk about all the past seasons of our family and the church. We've been through several Winters, Springs, Summers, and Falls together. On one of our walks, we were talking about the different seasons that women go through. I was sharing what a wonderful Springtime we were experiencing as new grandparents and how it is one of the best seasons of life. He said, "You should write a book about the seasons of a woman's life because you've been through every season: a single woman, engaged, married, married with kids, and grandkids." I said, "That's easy for you to say. You're an amazing author and gifted speaker." He has written hundreds of sermons, articles, and books for the past thirty-six years.

Over the next two weeks, when I walked the ocean lined path, I reflected on the seasons of my life, my career as a pastor's wife, and my marriage to David for thirty-six years. I was reminded I could not control the seasons I've been through, but I could choose to believe God's promises during my seasons. I started thinking about all the wonderful, strong women I've known over my lifetime.

My nine sisters and the women in my church family have all made a great impact on my life. My mother, Helen, mother-in-law, Sue, and my pastor's wife, Shirley Cannistraci, are a few of the women who have inspired me to write *Unexpected Seasons*.

Have you ever wondered why God has allowed certain things to happen in your life? Does your world seem to be out of control and chaotic? Have you had any of these thoughts: "Why is this happening to me? Is there some purpose to the challenges I'm facing? Am I doing what God wants me to do? Shouldn't I be married by now? Why did I get married?" Are you getting tired of waiting to see progress and fruit in your life? You're not alone. I've asked most of these questions; especially, "Why is this happening to ME?!"

One of the greatest benefits of being a Christian woman is you have a relationship with a God who loves you. You know that He has a purpose for every season in your life and has good plans for your future. He wants you to understand that through every season, He will be right by your side guiding every step.

In the book of Ecclesiastes, it says that there is a meaning and a purpose to everything that women go through in their lives. Ecclesiastes 3:1 says: "To everything there is a season, a time for every purpose under heaven."

The purpose of this book is to look at the spiritual seasons of a woman's life. You'll see how God reveals His purpose and plan through the Winter, Spring, Summer, and Fall seasons. His plan is to develop you and make you fruitful in every one of them. The different seasons are designed to strengthen you, as well as to instruct you in the ways of God. You shouldn't fear the changing seasons or the winds of adversity that blow through your life because your roots will grow deep when the winds are strong. The changing of the seasons will help you grow through a variety of time frames and conditions that you face in your life.

I grew up in a house with nine sisters and three brothers. I watched my sisters go through all the seasons of life. We saw every hairstyle from the bouffant teased hair of the sixties to the straight, long hair in the seventies and the big hair of the eighties. Boyfriends came and went. Then came the husbands, weddings, and children. You can only imagine, with ten girls living in the same house together, how much makeup, hair spray, and estrogen was flowing throughout our household. No wonder my dad worked a lot of overtime and played as much tennis as possible. My mom and dad had to go through every stage of life with their girls: every graduation, every boyfriend, every heartache, and every divorce. Looking back over the changing seasons of my childhood, my teenage years, my young adult life, being a wife, mother, and grandmother, I am convinced Jesus loves me and has had His hand in all my seasons. He has strengthened my life and my faith has grown.

Being a pastor's wife of the same church community for forty years has given me a unique perspective on the challenges that women face every day. I've had the honor of walking with the women that I love through the changing seasons of life. Recently, I've had conversations with women who are facing heart problems, chemo treatments, marriage challenges, divorce recoveries, surgeries to remove cancerous tumors, husbands who are addicted to heroin, long-term unemployment, parents who have overdosed on drugs, children who have all kinds of mental and physical challenges, loss of children and spouses, and the list goes on.

I've been inspired by the godly examples of these women as they walk through their difficulties and continue to trust God through the cold, stormy seasons. They are the true heroes of faith. I am continually amazed at their growth and faith in God, even during their Winter seasons.

As you read through this book, I hope you will be inspired by the stories of not only the women of the Bible, but also the amazing women I have been privileged to know for the last forty years. I believe their stories will encourage you to press on in your relationship with God. I hope they will motivate you to be patient and keep planting seeds of love and faith for your future harvest.

If you have picked up this book in the coldest Winter of your life be patient, God has an awesome future ahead for you. He wants to speak to your heart and give you a clear understanding of your unexpected seasons.

1
UNDERSTANDING NATURAL AND SPIRITUAL SEASONS

If we don't change, we don't grow.
If we don't grow, we aren't really living.

Gail Sheehy

I recently turned fifty-nine years old and I'm in a Spring Season as I write this book. That means new things and new opportunities are happening in my life. I am the grandmother of two boys and two girls, Liam is four, Asher is two, Chloe is three and Mila is one month. All grandparents know the "falling-in-love-again" feeling that happens when our children have their own children. It's that same "puppy-love feeling" that happens the first time you fall in love, only better!

I wish as a sixteen-year-old I knew what I know now, that seasons end, and new ones follow them. With every passing season, God has given me more understanding of His wonderful purpose for my life.

Maybe you're in a time or season of your life that makes it hard for you to believe that God wants to give you abundance and bring new opportunities your way. But I encourage you to begin to believe God will bring you into your season of blessing as you read the stories of ordinary women throughout this book. He not only wants to bring you to a place of favor but to a place of doing good works for others.

It's recorded in the book of 2 Corinthians that "God is able to make all grace abound (every favor and earthly blessing) come in abundance to you, so that you may always [under all circumstances, regardless of the need] have complete sufficiency in everything [being completely self-sufficient in Him] and have an abundance for every good work and act of charity" (2 Corinthians 9:8, AMP).

Seasons Change

In the early years of our marriage, my husband and I were blessed with our two-year-old son, Aaron, and I was three months pregnant with our second son, Jordan. We had just celebrated our fifth wedding anniversary; those first years of marriage were a big time of adjustment for me—learning how to be a new wife and mother was challenging to say the least.

Have you ever been in a time of your life when you're just getting comfortable with one season, then before you knew it, the next season was upon you? Can you relate to being overwhelmed with new and different challenges you have faced in different seasons of your life? I was in one of those seasons of change—adjusting as a young wife with a small child, taking care of a husband, pregnant again, laundry piled up, the mortgage bill due, the house needed to be cleaned and dinners needed to be cooked. Add to that a full-time job outside of the home and my husband is the pastor of a thriving church where church members want answers to life's most difficult questions—twenty-four hours a day, seven days a week.

I knew at this point in my marriage that my husband had a close relationship with Jesus and dreamed of accomplishing great things for God. He is the go-getter, visionary type, who is not satisfied unless he finishes what God wants Him to do. He tested out of high school at sixteen years of age and earned his Ph.D. degree by age twenty-nine. Pretty amazing guy, huh? He is the kind of man who spends a lot of time in prayer and one day he came to me and said, "I've been praying about something and I need to talk to you about it."

I was totally shocked by the disturbing news he gave me because it involved a huge change in our lifestyle. He couldn't have picked a worse time to share this news with me because I was in the first trimester of my pregnancy with symptoms of nausea, exhaustion and hormonal mood swings—crying one minute and laughing the next. When my husband said, "Hey, I have some exciting news for you—we're going on an adventure." To me, this wasn't exciting news at all. He might as well have said, "Hey, pack all of your belongings, we're flying on a spaceship to the moon." His proposal scared me so much that my stomach clenched with fear. This adventure, as he called it, was not the vision I had for my life. I thought I must be in a middle of a dream—because this happens to other women, not to me, "Somebody please pinch me and wake me up from this nightmare!" I'll fill you in on the rest of this story in the coming pages, so stay with me. But for now, let me ask you:

Have you ever received unexpected news and felt like you were hit upside the head with a bat? That's exactly how I felt, and this was a problem I couldn't handle on my own. I asked God, "Why are you doing this to me?" How could my husband be experiencing excitement over his new revelation from God while I was feeling the exact opposite? What would this change mean for my children's future? I don't do well with change, especially when it's not the plan I had for my life. Why would my husband ask me to do something I'm obviously not trained to do? Are you kidding me? Haven't I had enough change being a new mom, wife, and pastor? I told him, "I don't want to consider it, pray about it, and I never want to discuss it again." I'm usually an easy-going person, but go on this adventure—NO, that's not ever going to happen!

If only I understood at the young age of twenty-eight the great plans God had for my life and where He wanted to take me. He was trying to get me to a place of understanding His ways, His blessing, and favor. Looking back at that time in my life, I am now able to see: every season of change has a God-ordained purpose.

"Seek His will in all you do, and He will show you which path to take" (Proverbs 3:6, NLT).

"For My thoughts are not your thoughts, nor are your ways My ways, declares the Lord, for as the heavens are higher than the earth, so are My ways higher than your ways and My thoughts than your thoughts" (Isaiah 55:8-9, NIV).

I now know He was trying to guide me into a higher way of thinking and living. In the following chapters, I will share some thoughts on how God often performed miracles in my heart as I put my trust in Him during tumultuous seasons of change. We will discover how God reveals His wonderful plan for our lives through the beauty of creation and how we can understand His purpose in every changing season.

A Purpose to Every Season

In the Bible, we see that God is a God of order and He uses patterns and principles to show us how we can be fruitful in every season. One pattern God uses to guide us is the pattern of natural seasons. There are many spiritual seasons we will experience, and some seasons last longer than others. For example, you may be in a Winter season in your spiritual life and a Spring season in your career.

Solomon, the wisest man to ever live, explained it this way:

"To everything there is a season, a time for every purpose under heaven" (Ecclesiastes 3:1, KJV).

God wants you to understand that He manages every season in your life to accomplish His purposes. He will show you His plan through the natural beauty of creation. He changes the natural seasons four times in each year, along with the colors, the temperature, and the feel in the atmosphere. The process is all about the changing seasons of Winter, Spring, Summer, and Fall, and God controls it all. I will share how you can understand God's unfolding and purpose for your life in the following chapters.

"You own the day, you own the night; you put the stars and sun in place. You laid out the four corners of the earth, <u>shaped the seasons</u> of Summer and Winter" (Psalm 74:17, MSG).

Every season is designed to get you deeply rooted in your relationship with Him and bring you into a fruitful lifestyle. Your seasons are designed to instruct, strengthen, and prosper you in the ways of God. The Word of God says you will be fruitful in every season when you're planted in Him.

Psalm 1:3 says every woman that is "...planted by the streams of water...; will never wither...; but will always prosper."

Sometimes it's hard to believe God's promise of prosperity when we're in the heat of a Summer storm or in the subzero temperatures of Winter. It's difficult for us to envision a time in our lives that we will be successful because of our past mistakes or even our current circumstances. We all have difficulty understanding why we must go through cold, dark seasons, but you and I can discover, as we search the promises of God, how to be fruitful in every season of our lives.

"That person is like a tree <u>planted</u> by streams of water, which yields its fruit in its <u>season</u>, and whose leaf does not wither. Whatever they do <u>prospers</u>" (Psalm 1:1-3, NIV).

God makes a promise in the book of Psalms to every woman who is planted by His river. Women who put their total trust in God don't have to worry when the seasons change or the winds of adversity blow against them. When she is planted, watered and nourished by Him she need not fear that she will wither during the hot Summer... **whatever she does... shall prosper...** Let that sink in and meditate on the following promise God has made to you.

"Blessed is the one who trusts in the Lord, and whose hope is the Lord. For he shall be like a tree planted by the waters, which spreads out its roots by the river, and will not fear when heat comes; but its leaf will be green and will not be anxious in the year of drought, nor will cease from yielding fruit" (Jeremiah 17:7-8, NKJV).

Your Leaves are Green

This past year our church prayed for God to send rain to California during our four-year drought. We were desperate for water because our lakes, ponds, and waterways were all dried out. Our local water company sent out warnings not to use water on certain days and we had to ration what we did use. So, of course, the houses that had beautiful, green landscapes were now filled with wilting plants and dead flowers.

In the month of March God finally answered our prayers and we had record rains that flooded many streets in our neighborhoods. The water came rushing down over the mountains and filled the Anderson Dam behind my house. When the drought finally ended, I noticed the beautiful green hills and budding blossoms on the cherry trees near my home. They make me think about the variety of trees God uses to describe the woman who puts her trust in the Lord. Even when she goes through a dry season, her leaves stay green and she never ceases to yield fruit.

Understanding God's pattern of natural seasons gives us insight into our spiritual seasons. When I was sixteen years old, I was looking in all the wrong places for love and fulfillment. I was hoping that something or someone could quench my thirsty soul. I'm so thankful Jesus went out of His way to meet me during my personal season of drought.

I was reading a story about a woman who was searching for someone to love her, too. She just wanted to be understood and accepted. She thought a boyfriend could fill her empty love tank. After going through one lover after another, she was left empty-handed. I can relate to this woman because I also looked to men to fill the gaping hole in my heart—only to find I needed something more. I was emotionally empty and desperately needed God to fill me with His love and to heal my broken heart.

Give Me a Drink

The Apostle John tells of a place where Jesus stopped to get a drink of water at Jacob's well. There Jesus had a remarkable conversation with a Samaritan woman who came to the well to draw water. In this conversation, we learn that Jesus understood much about her heart and wanted to fill her with His everlasting love.

John gives the background of this divine appointment in John 4:1-30. Jesus chose the direct route on His way to Galilee, traveling through Samaria. Because of the prejudice against the Samaritans, many Jews journeyed almost twice the distance on a hotter and more uncomfortable road to get to Galilee. But Jesus cut right through that prejudice and went through Samaria.

The woman that Jesus met was in a spiritually dry place in her life, but her season was about to change. She was surprised that a Jewish rabbi would speak to a Samaritan woman like her—because of the great racial and cultural tensions of that day. Rabbis were never to talk to women in public—not even their wives or sisters. She was painfully aware that the Jews had no dealings with the Samaritans, especially an outcast like her. A woman like her would be looked down upon in her own community because she had been married five times and had a live-in lover at the time she met Jesus. She was in a place of feeling unloved, misunderstood, and unsupported. She was desperately trying to quench her spiritual thirst with a long list of men.

She was looked down upon in so many ways. First, she was an adulterer and a Samaritan woman at that. Samaritans were regarded by the Jews as half-breeds and reprobates. No wonder she was surprised when Jesus addressed her. Although there was another well in the village, as a moral outcast, she had to walk half a mile away in heat of the day.

After he asks for a drink of water, Jesus gets right to the point and explains why He is talking to her. It's not only because He's thirsty, but He uses the encounter at the well to speak directly to her broken heart. She came to the well to get her daily water. Instead, she encountered the One who could give her the living water that would quench her thirsty soul.

He was the answer to all her needs—her emptiness, confusion, and pain. She didn't know that He was the Messiah, but He makes it clear that He is the only one who can give her living water—the fountain that springs up into everlasting life. (John 4:14)

Many women I've talked to often feel unloved and misunderstood like the Samaritan woman. Maybe you feel unloved and misunderstood by the people in your family, church or community. And you've looked to other sources than God—men, money, houses, jobs—to fill your need to be loved, understood, and fulfilled.

Jesus wants you and me to know He completely understands our suffering because He has been human just like us. He passionately loves, continually supports, and perfectly understands us. Jesus wants us to know that we can be healed by His love and mercy. In the following verses, we see that He came to help us.

"It's obvious, of course, that he didn't go to all this trouble for angels. It was for people like us, children of Abraham. That's why he had to enter into every detail of human life. He would have already experienced it all himself–all the pain, all the testing–and would be able to help where help was needed" (Hebrews 2:16-18, MSG).

On that blessed day, Jesus came to the well to get a drink of water, He knew what it would take to heal the Samaritan woman. He said: "If you knew about the gift of God and Who it is that is saying to you, give Me a drink, you would have asked of Him and He would have given you living water."

She was desperately seeking what every woman longs for: to be understood and loved. The men in her life were not able to give the love she needed. Jesus revealed the secret to her satisfaction. The gift of God that He is speaking about is the Holy Spirit—the living water is the only thing that can satisfy her.

"Jesus answered and said to her, if you knew the gift of God, and Who it is who says to you, Give me a drink. You would have asked Him, and He would have given you living water" (John 4:10, NASB).

Whenever Jesus speaks Words of life into the heart of a confused woman with five husbands or a young teenager, who is lost and alone, He satisfies their thirsty souls with His everlasting fountain.

Jesus answered and said to her,

"Everyone who drinks of this water will thirst again; but whoever drinks of the water that I will give him shall never thirst; but whoever drinks of the water that I will give him shall never thirst; but the water that I will give him will become in him a well of water springing up to eternal life. The woman said to Him, Sir give me this water, so I will not be thirsty, nor come all the way here to draw" (John 4: 13-15, NIV).

Ask Him to Water You Today

Just like the Samaritan woman I encountered Jesus' love as a teenager. I found out that He loves me even though He knows everything about me. God's promises never change even though we're imperfect. I had a choice to make—I could go on living in a dry and thirsty place like most of my teenage friends or I could choose to let Him fill me with His living water, so I would never have to be thirsty again.

At that moment, I didn't understand there were many seasons ahead of me, that I would need His loving support and understanding. I have learned over the last forty years—every time I get thirsty, I can ask Him for a drink from His living fountain.

As you journey through every season, remember, blessed is the woman who trusts in the Lord.

"Blessed is the one who trusts in the Lord, and whose hope is the Lord" (Jeremiah 17:7, NKJV).

"And I will always guide you and satisfy you with good things. I will keep you strong and well. You will be like a garden that has plenty of water, like a spring of water that never goes dry"

(Isaiah 58:11, GNT).

I would like to encourage you to envision yourself as a well-watered garden. Ask God to make you a woman who puts her full trust in God and believe that He will continually guide you through every changing season.

Discussion Questions

Open Up: Did you ever have a time or a season in your life that made it hard to believe God wanted to give you an abundant life?

Share Scriptures: Let different members/friends share a verse or an idea from this chapter that impacted them personally. What does it mean for you?

Talk It Over: How does understanding seasons help you to understand your season?

Pray Together: Pray for each other to trust God during your seasons.

Prayer for Understanding Seasons:

Father God, your word says you will guide me during my season of drought. Thank You for strengthening me and making me a well-watered garden as I trust you.

2
IT'S COLD OUTSIDE

Have you ever been through a personal Winter? Winter brings a time of cold, harsh weather; it's rainy, cold, and gray. In many places Winter brings sub-zero temperatures, snow, and ice; the sun isn't shining and there's no warmth outside. Everything seems dead and nothing is growing. Even God may seem distant and cold. What do we want to do in Winter? We want to stay out of the cold and find a place to be warm and cozy, hopefully in front of a blazing fireplace, under a warm blanket—reading a good book. We just want to hibernate and hope for Springtime to come.

So many women have walked through a cold, personal Winter season—possibly with a loss of a loved one, a divorce, or loss of a job or a business. You and I can't control our season, but we can choose to believe God's promises during a Winter season.

"But the Word is very near you, in your mouth and in your heart, that you may do it. See, I have set before you today to love the Lord your God, to walk in His ways, and to keep His commandments. His statutes, and His judgments, that you may live and multiply; and the Lord your God will bless you in the land which you go to possess" (Deuteronomy 30:14, NASB).

A TIME TO DREAM

Winter is a time to dream, plan, and to believe for the good things God has for your future harvest. During the natural Winter season, a farmer begins to think about a future harvest and he dreams about the seed he'll plant and the return for his efforts. He focuses on new possibilities and opportunities. In the same way, you need to allow the Holy Spirit to impart a fresh new dream and direction for your life.

"A man has joy by the answer of his mouth, and a word spoken in due season, how good it is" (Proverbs 15:23, NKJV).

He is our heavenly father Who desires to have a loving relationship with us, to guide us through our Winter season. God is a talker and wants to reveal His purpose in our seasons. There are several ways that God communicates with us. One way is through dreams. Look at the following examples:

"Then in my dream, the angel of God said to me, Jacob! And I replied, Yes, here I am" (Genesis 31:11, NLT).

"In the first year of Belshazzar king of Babylon, Daniel had a dream, and visions passed through his mind as he was lying in bed" (Daniel 7:1, NIV).

"Then he had another dream, and he told it to his brothers...Soon, Joseph had another dream, and again he told his brothers about it" (Genesis 37:9, NIV).

"Each of us had a dream the same night, and each dream had a meaning of its own" (Genesis 41:11, NIV).

God spoke to many people through dreams to give them direction for their future. In the New Testament God spoke to Joseph in a dream that Mary was pregnant with the Messiah.

"But while He thought about these things, behold, an angel of the Lord appeared to him in a dream. Joseph, son of David, do not be afraid to take to you, Mary your wife, for that which is conceived in her is of the Holy Spirit. And she will bring forth a son, Jesus, for He will save His people from their sins" (Matthew 1:20-21, NKJV).

On the day of Pentecost, the Apostle Peter referred to Amos the prophet. He said that God would speak to men of maturity through dreams.

"In the last days, God says, I will pour out my Spirit on all people. Your sons and daughters will prophesy, your young man will see visions, your old men will dream dreams" (Acts 2:17, NIV).

Job said that God speaks to us while we're in a deep sleep, when we're totally quiet when He can get our undivided attention.

"For God does speak—now one way, now another—though no one perceives it. In a dream, in a vision of the night, when deep sleep falls upon people as they slumber in their beds" (Job 33:14-15, NIV).

A Time to Hear from God

A dream is a mental picture or a vision of a future reality imparted by God. Dreams are an essential part of life. A person never achieves more than their dreams. When you dream, you are seeing beyond the limitations of now. When you dream you open yourself to a future on the other side of your mountain:

"For truly, I say to you, if you have faith like a grain of mustard seed, you will say to this mountain, "Move from here to there, 'and it will move, and nothing will be impossible to you*"* (Matthew 17:20, ESV).

Mountain-moving faith starts with a dream, an idea of what could be. You don't have to stay stuck in a cold Winter rut. A Winter dream shapes the future and gives you the power of hope in the present. Winter may seem negative, but it is actually a very positive season in God. It is a time to be inspired by God to dream again. It is meant to be a time of hearing from God. In fact, did you know that the revelation you get in Winter, releases Springtime?

"He spreads snow like a white fleece, he scatters frost like ash, who can survive his Winter? Then he gives the command and it all melts; he breathes on Winter—suddenly it's Spring" (Psalm 147:17-18, MSG).

It's a big mistake to let Winter pass without redeeming the time and preparing for your future harvest.

"The lazy man will not plow because of <u>Winter</u>: He will beg during harvest and have nothing" (Proverbs 20:4, NKJV).

When Our Dreams Die

What about when our dreams seem to die in our Winter season? In the last few years, the world has gone through its own Winter Season. Every day we seem to hear of another mass killing or bombing. Some think the American dream has turned into the American nightmare and there is a growing fear. You might even be in your own personal Winter.

Pastor Jim Johnson gave the following message to his church, Reset, Berlin Germany, August 28, 2016)

> I was very surprised yesterday at how emotional I became during my message. Over the decades I have been preaching, there are not more than a couple of times that my message involved tears and the inability to speak without a broken voice. Yesterday I simply broke as I spoke to our church about the brokenness of this world, the unthinkable violence that is now commonplace and the overwhelming weight of darkness people are buried under in the world today.
>
> The statistics are off the charts. One suicide every 40 seconds (projected to be 1 every 20 seconds by the year 2020), 1,142 acts of terrorism in 2016 (through August 24th) with at least 11,192 people

being killed. Truly the Scripture from Isaiah 60:2 fits, "See, darkness covers the earth and thick darkness is over the peoples," But there is hope in this dark and broken world. Here is Isaiah's proclamation, 60:1-3 "Arise, shine, for your light has come, and the glory of the Lord rises upon you. See, darkness covers the earth and thick darkness is over the peoples, but the Lord rises upon you and his glory appears over you. Nations will come to your light, and kings to the brightness of your dawn.

It seems like many women are going through their own personal Winters. But God wants to speak hope and vision into your most difficult challenges. The glory of the Lord will rise on you again, even though there is darkness everywhere.

This past year I have prayed with women who have lost their babies through miscarriages and sickness. Others have lost loved ones and are in a time of grief. It reminds me of the story of Naomi and Ruth, two women in the Bible who lost their husbands and experienced Winter seasons.

Naomi was a widow who thought God had abandoned her in the coldest time of her life. She had to watch those she loved wither and die in a terrible famine. She lost both of her sons and her husband, Elimelech. She said:

"The Lord Himself has raised his fist against me" (Ruth 1:13, NLT).

She had no choice but to move back to a place where God was providing for his people. She moved from the land of Moab back to her homeland of Judah. She heard that the Lord had caused Judah to prosper and produce food for His people. She told her daughters-in-law, that she had nothing to offer them, nowhere to live or wealth to inherit. There were no other sons for them to marry. Naomi was in a Winter for sure. Have you ever felt like Naomi? She was in the middle of nowhere, feeling totally alone and left with nothing. She and Ruth were greeted by Naomi's friends when they arrived at her childhood home. When her friends saw her, they greeted her as Naomi.

"Don't call me Naomi [pleasant]; call me Mara [bitter], for the Almighty has dealt very bitterly with me. I went out full, but the Lord has brought me home again empty" (Ruth 1:20-21, AMP).

At this point in her life, she was looking through the dark-colored eyeglasses of pain. Her bitterness was coloring her view of God and what He wanted to do for her future.

God Raised His Fist Against Her

How can you imagine a great future harvest when tragedy happens? What should we do when our dreams seem to die in our Winter season? When Naomi felt that '**God had raised His fist against her**' and she was in a cold Winter season, not knowing where her next meal was coming from, she went back to the place where she would be supported. At this time in her life, she couldn't see any hope for her family's future, but God indeed had a wonderful plan.

In her early life she knew God to be a God of blessing, but now she was in deep despair, seeing only her natural circumstances—no sons—no grandchildren—no future—no hope. She had no faith whatsoever. But it's interesting when her friends saw her they said, "Is that Naomi, is that the pleasant person we knew in our childhood?" God was about to take her through a wonderful healing process. Her Winter season would not last forever—Springtime was right around the corner!

Childhood Sweethearts

Tim and Cari were childhood sweethearts. They got married right out of high school when they were both 18-years-old. Like all newly married couples, they had big dreams for their future. They started a family with their first little girl, then their second daughter was born. They moved from Northern California to Southern California to be on a team that pioneered a start-up church. Tim already had a few years of experience working with teenagers in his previous church. So, it was easy for him to continue working with the Youth Ministry in his new church. Cari was also heavily involved and did anything it took to make this new church a success. They also opened a new business together. They were so excited to be working together to build the Kingdom of God, their family, and their new business.

One day a fire broke out in the hills behind their home. Before they knew it, it was raining ash outside and their entire neighborhood had to be evacuated. Tim was talking to Cari about all the blessings that God had given their little family. He rehearsed all their accomplishments. He said I have a great job, a wonderful wife, our first home together, the car, two beautiful girls. Cari said, "Tim, this isn't really the time to be rehearsing our blessings, we've been told we have to leave our home and evacuate; we don't really have time to have this conversation." A week prior to the fire, Tim told Cari that he had just added more life insurance to his existing policy and told her that she and the girls would be covered. He said, "If something happens to me, I want you to move on, don't cry over me. I want you and the girls to be happy." Little did Cari know, a week later, would be the last time she would talk to Tim.

They all evacuated, but the men of the neighborhood stayed behind to help the firemen. Tim was riding a motorized scooter around the neighborhood to make sure people were safe. His scooter stumbled over a rock that launched him into the air and he fell and hit his head. A Christian man found him lying on the side of the road and prayed over him. Tim was then taken to the hospital. He was on life support in the hospital for nine days and then passed on to his heavenly home.

They were married seven and a half years. Can you imagine? One day you're happily married to your childhood sweetheart and the next day he's gone? She believed that he would be healed, only to be told he was gone. Have you ever felt like you were all alone and by yourself? Cari knew that they would never grow old together and Tim wouldn't have the joy of seeing his girls get married and have his grandchildren. Even though Cari felt alone and abandoned, she knew that God had good plans for her family's future. She knew that God would one day give her the supernatural strength to dream again.

Cari told me she read the story in the Bible about Ruth and Naomi repeatedly. She saw that her story was like the one in the book of Ruth. She held onto God's promises in His Word in the following months with everything that was within her; trusting God to see her through this terrible Winter.

Because Cari is a person who enjoys putting together teachings and sermons for her church, she knew what it was to research the Bible for answers. She saw that God was a restorer and found that God not only restores a person to their previous state, but He answers their prayers. He gave her exceedingly, abundantly, more than she could ask or think... God restored Cari to a place of peace... better than she had before.

Cari saw when God began the restoration process for Naomi—He blessed her with a loving daughter-in-law, Ruth, and her entire community. He gave Ruth a wealthy husband, Boaz, who provided everything that their family needed. God blessed Naomi above and beyond her wildest dreams, and a grandson was born. God had chosen Ruth to give birth in the family line of the Messiah!

Boaz is a picture and a symbol of the redeeming work of Jesus. I don't know if you know it, but Jesus and Boaz have a lot in common. Boaz assumed the duties of his family and was willing to pay the complete price for Ruth and Naomi's restoration. (Ruth 4:12-17)

Jesus paid the price for you on the cross to be totally healed and restored. He is your Redeemer and the healer of your broken dreams. He wants to restore your joy and bring you into a wonderful harvest season.

My Mouth Was Filled with Laughter

Cari said that if someone told her that God was going to bless her with more than what she lost, she wouldn't have believed it. That's why it was so important for her to begin to dream again and look to God for her provision. She read this story over and over because she couldn't really picture a time when she wouldn't be in pain. She said, "I will always have the reality that Tim is gone and that he is never coming back." She saw how God took Naomi's pain and transitioned her pain into hope. She said, "It will feel like a dream when I'm not crying and filled with so much sorrow. If it weren't for holding on to God's promises, I don't know how I could ever have moved forward. I had to believe, more than anything, that God's promises are true."

She based her hope and expectation in God and believed she would be restored. She would say to herself, "Someday I'm going to laugh and really enjoy my life." God had begun to give her excitement for the future. She said, "My heart would hurt every day and I would feel the pain." She knew that God was taking her through a process and little by little, He was healing her heart. She would thank God every day for His provision. She chose to believe that He was going to deliver her from her pain and sorrow. Cari couldn't control the season she was in, but she chose to believe God's promises for her future.

Cari was my husband's assistant before she and Tim moved to Southern California. When Tim passed away, she asked God if

He would provide a job for her back in San Jose, and if possible, open a door for her to work for Pastor David again. She would know that God was directing her to move back to San Jose and be close to her immediate family if that came to pass. Through a series of events, she did move back to San Jose and is currently working as the Executive Assistant to Pastor David. Cari is an amazing, loving person and a joy to work alongside—we couldn't do it without her! She has moved into a bigger and better house with her girls and is laughing again!

"When the Lord brought back the captivity of Zion, we were like those who dream. Then our mouth was filled with laughter, And our tongue with singing. Then they said among the nations, The Lord has done great things for them. The Lord has done great things for us, and we are glad" (Psalm 126:1-3, NKJV).

No matter what the reasons are for your Winter season, feeling like you have lost everything and you're all alone, God can give you a dream for your future. You might feel that you will be in the Winter season forever and that you'll never laugh again or find enjoyment. God wants you to dream again. He will speak to you in your night season and guide you into your next season.

"I will bless the Lord who has given me counsel; yes, my heart instructs me in the night seasons" (Psalm 16:7, AMP).

Naomi could have stayed blinded by her bitterness, but little by little she could see that God was providing for her. God's plan was bigger than Naomi could have ever imagined. She couldn't see how God wanted to take care of her every need. But in His goodness, He used Ruth, Boaz, her friends and community to give her hope. Once again, He made her fruitful.

Then the women of the town said to Naomi [pleasant], "Praise the Lord, who has now provided a redeemer for your family! May this child be famous in Israel. May he restore your youth and care for you in your old age. For he is the son of your daughter-in-law who loves you and has been better to you than seven sons" (Ruth 4:14-15, NLT)!

Sometimes you might not be able to see that God has a plan to prosper you during your pain and suffering, but He wants you to dream again and open your eyes to the new possibilities you have in Him.

STEPS TO DREAMING AGAIN

Let me share some positive ways you can let the Holy Spirit restore your joy and give you hope for your future.

A Time to be Quiet

Get away from distractions. Set aside alone time for dreaming. Relax and be quiet. We need to still our minds and listen for God to speak His plans and purpose for our lives. We will know it is God's voice because it will be supportive, loving, and positive. The enemy's voice is condemning, fearful, and negative.

"Be still and know that I am God; I will be exalted among the nations, I will be exalted in the earth" (Psalm 46:10, NIV).

"For I know the plans I have for you, says the Lord, they are plans for good and not to disaster, to give you a future and a hope" (Jeremiah 29:11, NLT).

Set Your Mind on Lovely Things

Think positively about the future. Look beyond the struggle of the daily grind and think about what lies ahead. Ask yourself, "What kind of person do I want to be, and what things do I want to do with my life? What would I do if resources were unlimited and anything was possible?" Believe that you can rise above your circumstances and see life from a positive and encouraging perspective.

"Since, then, you have been raised with Christ, set your hearts on things above, where Christ is seated at the right hand of God. Set your minds on things above, not on earthly things" (Colossians 3:1-2, NIV).

"Finally, brothers and sisters, whatever is true, whatever is noble, whatever is right, whatever is pure, whatever is lovely, whatever is admirable—if anything is excellent or praiseworthy--think about such things" (Philippians 4:8, NIV).

Ask the Holy Spirit to Reveal His Dream for Your Life

"When the Holy Spirit, who is truth, comes, he shall guide you into all truth, for he will not be presenting his own ideas, but will be passing on to you what he has heard. He will tell you about the future" (John 16:13, TLB).

"You can ask for anything in My Name, and I will do it, so that the Son can bring glory to the Father" (John 14:13, NLT).

Because you are connected to the Name of Jesus and you belong to Him, you can ask anything in His Name. He said, "He will do it for you." Ask the Holy Spirit to reveal God's dream for your life. You can be what God wants you to be and you can do what God wants you to do. Search the Scriptures and identify with people of faith who overcame similar circumstances.

Expect Him to Answer

"For surely there is an end; and your expectation shall not be cut off," (Proverbs 23:18, AKJ).

"Call to Me, and I will answer you and tell you great and unsearchable things you do not know" (Jeremiah 33:3, NIV).

Define Your Dreams

Write down your calling based on your gifting, personality, and passion. What you hear God speaking to you through His Word and the Holy Spirit will guide you into your next season.

"Make a careful exploration of who you are and the work you have been given, and then sink yourself into that. Don't be impressed with yourself. Don't compare yourself with others. Each of you must take responsibility for doing the creative best you can with your own life" (Galatians 6:4-5, MSG).

Clarify and define your dream, using plenty of paper. This is how you can remember and hold on to it. As time goes on, it will be refined and clarified if you don't let go of it.

"And the Lord answered me and said, Write the vision; make it plain on tablets, so he may run who reads it" (Habakkuk 2:2, ESV).

Believe for New Things

"Abraham believed in the God who brings the dead back to life and who creates new things of our nothing" (Romans 4:17, NLT).

Things may seem cold, dead, and lifeless, but God can bring back your laughter and the joy of living. God has not finished your story yet. Just like Cari and Naomi, their dreams didn't stop in the dead of Winter; God had a heavenly plan for their lives. Your story is not over because there are other seasons ahead and a greater plan going on in heavenly places for you.

"I will never lay aside your laws, for you have used them to restore my joy and my health" (Psalm 119:93, TLB).

Discussion Questions

Remember: What we hear in Winter releases our Spring and becomes the foundation of our future harvest.

Open Up: How can a dream guide you in your Winter season?

Share Scriptures: Let different members/friends share a verse or idea from this chapter that impacted them personally. What does it mean for you?

Talk It Over: How did Cari make it through her Winter season? How can you begin to dream again?

Pray Together: Pray for each other and ask the Holy Spirit to reveal His dreams for your lives.

Prayer for the Winter Seasons:

Dear Holy Spirit, thank You for Your guidance and direction during my Winter Season. I believe You are going to answer me and give me a vision for my future harvest.

3
IT'S SPRINGTIME

For everything there is a season. A time to plant
And a time to harvest.
Ecclesiastes 3:1-2 (NLT)

Spring is a beautiful time of the year because the earth bursts forth with wildflowers and we hear the birds singing. Spring is the time of year when the weather transitions from the cold season into warmer temperatures—it's a time to shed our sweaters and coats and change into our brightly colored clothing.

Spring is a time for farmers to begin working the soil and planting their seeds. The farmer wakes herself up from her Winter hibernation and believes her God-given dreams will become a reality.

For some, Spring is a time for daydreams, play, and an escape from reality. Spring brings feelings of excitement and joy. You may have heard of "Spring Fever" and "Spring Break."

"For lo, the <u>winter</u> is past, the rain is over and gone; the flowers appear in the earth; the time of singing of birds is come, and the voice of the turtle dove is heard in our land" (Song of Solomon 2:11-12, KJV).

In this chapter, we will discover that Spring is not only a time for playing, but it is a time for women to invest and move forward to assure their future harvest. It's a time of anticipating good things.

In the natural, Springtime brings new opportunities and new beginnings—a single woman planning to be married is likely to be in a Springtime of her life. A graduate ready to start her career, a church planter or business entrepreneur beginning a new project is entering a Spring season. Effective women develop their dreams and plans in the Winter, so they are ready to follow up with action in the Spring; they are taking responsibility for turning their plans into reality, not sitting idly by to wait for someone to hand it to them. You can let others help you, but only you have the responsibility for your harvest. Spring is ultimately about opportunity—it's a gift—a chance to step closer to God and be sensitive to what the Holy Spirit wants to do in your Spring season.

When my husband, David, and I purchased a home in Morgan Hill, California, we discovered that we were moving into a thriving farming community. A few miles from our home is a local pumpkin patch. I like to take my grandkids there to ride the kiddie train and let them experience the beauty of God's creation. It's a spectacular sight as we wander through the sixty- plus varieties of pumpkins—traditional orange, stripes, warts, colors, all in amazing shapes and sizes. Right across the street from my home is an orchard that grows many kinds of fruit. I was surprised to learn that the owner grows fifteen kinds of apricots, twenty-four flavors of nectarines, eighteen varieties of cherries, not to mention the dates, prunes, raisins, pistachios, and the delicious walnuts he sells.

Through the pages of Scripture, God paints a picture of the variety of fruitful trees that flourish and continue to bear fruit even in times of drought.

"Blessed is the man who trusts in the Lord and whose trust is the Lord. For he will be like a tree planted by the water, that extends its roots by a stream and will not fear when the heat comes; but its leaves will be green, and it will not be anxious in a year of drought nor cease to yield fruit" (Jeremiah 17:7-9, NIV).

Our lives can be as fresh and green—even in a spiritual drought— as the tree in the book of Jeremiah if we put our trust in the Lord. The deeper our roots extend in Him during the hot weather the stronger and more stable we become. As we faithfully plant seeds of God's Word in our Spring season, we will continue to be blessed and produce righteous fruit.

A TIME TO LOVE

Spring is a time when many young, engaged couples prepare for their weddings. Engagement is a wonderful time in a young couple's journey. They dream of building their future together. Love is in the air, the birds are singing, romantic songs are played, flowers are selected, photographers and caterers are reserved. It is as if the two lovebirds are magnetized to each other in every sense of the word. I love romance as much as anyone. After thirty-five years of marriage, I still sit across the table from my husband at restaurants just for the sheer enjoyment of gazing into his handsome golden eyes. Young engaged couples are in a springtime of their lives.

"I will sing for joy in God, explode in praise from deep in my soul! For as the earth bursts with Spring wildflowers, and as a garden cascades with blossoms, so the Master, God, brings righteousness into full bloom and puts praise on display before the nations*"* (Isaiah 61:10a-11, MSG).

We are going to meet some people in this chapter who have been through their Spring season and the steps they took to assure their future harvest.

A few months before my son Aaron's wedding, he asked me some heartfelt questions about love and marriage. He asked, "Mom, what things do I have to look forward to in the first year of my marriage?" So, being a good mother, I wanted to be sensitive to his Spring season, so I started off with the positive side of a young couple's first year. I told him, "Son, the first week, you will see rainbows, unicorns, and butterflies dancing outside the window of your new home. Marriage was created by God and it's a beautiful union between a man and a woman. It will be exciting to set up your new home just the way you like it. You and Carrie will make a great team because you work well together. You're both level-headed and will make good choices for your future."

Then, being a very practical and truthful person, I continued the conversation with a dose of reality. "Son, it's not always easy to love because marriages are constantly transitioning from one season of life to another. Love is an action—a verb. If you're going to have a good marriage, you must plant seeds of patience, long-suffering, and bear with one another's faults. (1 Corinthians 13:4-8) Then, as your family begins to grow, babies are added to your household and they wake up crying in the middle of the night, bills start coming and there is laundry to do." He said, "Mom, why are you telling me my marriage is going to stink?" I said, "Son, have I ever lied to you? Because I love you, I'm going to tell you the truth. If you follow the love chapter in 1 Corinthians 13 and plant seeds of love in your relationship, you'll reap a harvest of love."

It would be wonderful if we could just sit back, relax, and watch the flowers bloom in the Spring, but it's a time to get busy and plant.

"Let us not become weary in doing good, for at the proper time we will reap a harvest if we do not give up" (Galatians 6:9, NIV).

A Woman of Action

Women who desire to be fruitful are called to be 'doers' of God's Word. (James 1:22) We can't control our spiritual or natural seasons or what the weather conditions will be outside, but we can choose to put God's Word into action. Jesus was the greatest example of what it means to be a 'doer' when He came down from heaven to live among us. He hasn't only communicated His love with His Words, but He showed how much He loves us by the greatest act of all—He died for us.

The Apostle Peter summed up Jesus' life in a few words: "Jesus went around doing good deeds." Ladies, when we imitate Jesus and become 'doers' of what God reveals to us in our Spring season, we will bear fruit in all of our seasons. After all, a vision or a dream that comes from God becomes effective only when it is translated into action. We do our part, so He can do His part!

A Wise Woman

"The wise woman builds her house, but with her own hands the foolish one tears hers down" (Proverbs 14:1, NIV).

When I was a newlywed, I thought my husband's role in my life was to meet all my needs. I was a young woman with dreams of romance, chocolate covered strawberries, and preconceived ideas of what married life would bring me. Smile! I didn't realize that my marriage would be the place God would require me to be a 'doer' of the Word.

In the early years of my marriage, I learned that my bad behavior and selfish actions were not building my marriage. I grew up in a household where it was common to express our displeasure with unkind words. One time my husband and I were in a heated discussion—otherwise known as a fight. I know it's hard to believe, but I told him to "shut up." I immediately realized that the fruit that fell off that tree was rotten. Those two words were ugly, evil seeds. They didn't produce anything but dead, dried up fruit.

One morning in my daily devotions I read Proverbs 14:1 and discovered that a wise woman builds her house with her own hands. "Hands" in this verse speak of our behavior and our actions. Our good actions are the seeds that we sow and when they mature, we will eventually reap a harvest of blessings.

A friend once told me that wisdom means knowing the difference between right and wrong. She said wisdom gives you the skills for living correctly. After she shared that piece of advice with me, I was on a quest to make God's wisdom the foundation upon which to build my marriage.

"I, wisdom, will make the hours of your day more profitable and the years of your life more fruitful" (Proverbs 9:11, TLB).

Have you ever met a couple whose marriage has been happy for forty years and counting and they're still kind to one another? You can be sure they've gone through the cold of Winter, the excitement of Spring, the heat of Summer, and the colorful season of Fall. But because they have built their house on the wisdom of God, they are like the palm tree spoken of in Psalm 92:14 that says we can flourish and yield fruit in our old age.

"The righteous shall flourish like a palm tree, they shall grow like a cedar in Lebanon. Those who are planted in the house of the Lord shall flourish in the courts of our God. They shall still bear fruit in old age; they shall be fresh and flourishing" (Psalm 92:14, NKJV).

What does the writer of Psalms mean when he says, "[We] shall flourish like a palm tree?" It means the righteous woman will blossom, succeed, and do well because she is planted and deeply rooted in the house of the Lord. She will grow strong like a cedar of Lebanon, the California Redwood or the Giant Sequoia. These members of the cedar family are known for being precious wood. Many people in India and Lebanon have their furniture made from a cedar tree because it's strong and has a long life. A cedar tree can live up to a hundred years and redwoods live up to a thousand years. God wants us to blossom like palm trees and continue to bear fruit in our old age, just like a cedar tree.

Do you have a dream for a flourishing life that is filled with the fruit of the Spirit—love, joy, peace, patience, gentleness, goodness, kindness, self-control, and truthfulness? Ask God to give you wisdom and show you how to plant seeds of righteousness. His Word will teach you how to build your life with His wisdom. He said if you ask Him for wisdom, He will generously supply it. (James 1:6)

It's not always easy to plant seeds of love and put the Word of God into action when you don't feel like it. Sometimes it's difficult to ask God for His wisdom when you're having a bad day and you want your own way. Godly women who intentionally plant righteous seeds in their workplace, homes, and families will reap a fruitful harvest.

"You're blessed when you meet Lady Wisdom, when you make friends with Madame Insight. She's worth far more than money in the bank; her friendship is better than a big salary. Her value exceeds all the trappings of wealth; nothing you could wish for holds a candle to her. With one hand she gives long life, with the other she confers recognition. Her manner is beautiful, her life wonderfully complete. She's the very Tree of Life to those who embrace her. Hold her tight—and be blessed" (Proverbs 3:13-18, MSG)

DON'T DELAY – DO IT TODAY

The first rule of Springtime is: don't delay—do it TODAY! Be proactive, don't over-spiritualize it. Ladies, God will not do our planting for us. Things don't just happen as we sit around and wait for all of life's circumstances to be perfect.

"Farmers who wait for the perfect weather never plant. If they watch every cloud, they never harvest" (Ecclesiastes 1:4, NLT).

Procrastination is one of our greatest enemies. Women who tend to put off hard tasks until tomorrow never see their harvest.

You might be a procrastinator if:

- You tend to put off tasks or projects until the last minute
- You spend more time thinking than doing
- People are always chasing you for things you're supposed to do
- You are often late with projects or assignments

We all struggle with putting things off until tomorrow to one degree or another. But if we bring God into every challenging situation, He will give us the guidance and direction that we need.

Meditate on the following Bible passage in Proverbs—one of my favorites— and make the decision to include God in your Spring season. He promises to give you direction as you invite Him into every area of your life.

"In all your ways acknowledge Him, and He shall direct your paths" (Proverbs 3:6).

Each new day, as we endeavor to know Him better, we will experience new blessings in our life. God promises to direct our path as we have daily, intimate contact with Him. He will show you what to do, so go do it! Do not let the enemy of procrastination keep you from being a woman of action and a doer of the Word in all your seasons.

"Continue to work out your own salvation with fear and trembling, for it God who works in you to will and to act in order to fulfill his good purpose" (Philippians 2:12-13, NIV).

A Woman of War

A woman who is in her Spring season understands there is a right time for everything that happens in her life. 2 Samuel 11:1 (CEV) says, "Spring is the time when kings go to war." Most women don't think of themselves as warriors, but there are many battles we face in that season. If we're going to be an overcomer in the Spring, we must be willing to be trained to fight.

Fight the Enemy with the Truth

The biggest battle we face is the one that begins in our thought lives. A woman at church told me one day: "I just feel like I take two steps forward in one area of my life, then I get attacked in my thought life with the mistakes of my past." I said, "The enemy doesn't want you to make progress in your relationship with God. He uses lies to harass and distract you from moving forward. Satan would like nothing better than to keep you in a constant state of emotional turmoil. He wants you to believe that you can't be a strong, victorious woman."

If we're going to move forward in our relationship with God, we must fight the enemy with the truth of God's Word. One way to train ourselves is by making a choice to practice the promises of God daily. We overcome the war that rages against our minds by acknowledging we're in a spiritual battle.

The Apostle Paul says, "...our war is not against natural man, or the things we can see. But our war is against spiritual enemies that argue with God's true Word" (2 Corinthians 10:3-5). Negative thoughts contrary to God's Word can come against our minds want to keep us in a state of confusion and defeat.

Have you ever suffered through a spiritual battle that affected your thought patterns? How do you fight the enemy when he harasses your mind? It helps to understand that Satan is the father of lies and there is no truth in Him. (John 8:44)

Have you noticed when God highlights His Word in your mind, an opposing thought tries to overrule it? Let me give you an example: the very day I went to church and made the decision to follow Jesus, I was thrilled to know that God forgave me and wanted to give me a new life. But, I soon found out that Satan also had a plan for my life—to keep me captive to his ugly lies. He was right there whispering his awful lies into my spirit.

The book of Ephesians teaches us to use the Sword of the Spirit (the Word of God) when Satan tempts us with his lies. What is the Sword of the Spirit? When Jesus was on a forty day fast in Luke 4:3-13 he was led into the wilderness, full of the Holy Spirit. He wielded the Sword of the Spirit, the Word of God, against the devil. The Sword that he used was a specific, quickened Word from the Holy Spirit (a *Rhema* word). The devil came at Jesus and taunted him with his lies, questioning who He was.

The devil said, "If you're the Son of God turn these stones into bread." Jesus answered, "It is written, that man shall not live by bread alone, but by every Word of God." Like Jesus, you are equipped with every piece of God's armor, including the Sword of the Spirit. (Ephesians 6:10, 17). It is imperative that we know the Word, which is the truth.

The devil loves to whisper lies into our ears when we're down and discouraged, but Jesus gave us the Word of God, the Sword of the spirit, to fight all the attacks of the enemy. It is always good to be trained and prepared for a big fight. Hebrews 10:32 says that a spiritual battle, against your mind, usually follows a revelation from God.

"But recall the former days, in which, after you were illuminated, you endured a great struggle (fight) with sufferings" (Hebrews 10:32a, NKJV).

Listen to His Voice

"Incline your ear, and hear the words of the wise, and apply your heart to my knowledge" (Proverbs 22:17, NKJV.)

Another way God trains His daughters to fight is to listen to His voice. John 9:27 says, "My sheep listen to My voice; I know them, and they follow me." We need to listen to His voice, above every lying voice, and follow Him. He wants to give us insight into the spiritual realm and teach us how to fight our enemies. Ask Him to reveal Himself in every situation.

Imagine this scenario: you're taking time to read the Word of God and it says, "God loves you and whoever believes in Him will have everlasting life." (John 3:16) Then, a random thought or a lie from the enemy whispers, "No one loves you and you don't have everlasting life." This would be a typical lie that the enemy uses to harass a child of God.

Lying is the enemy's weapon of choice. When he assaults your mind with negative thoughts, fears, and doubt, remember what God has revealed to you in His Word. He will give you the ability to fight and overcome Satan's lies by placing the quickened Word in your hands and your heart.

The Word of God is living and powerful, and sharper than any two-edged sword, piercing even to the division of soul and spirit, and of joints and marrow, and is a discerner of the thoughts and intents of the heart. (Hebrews 4:12) A good portion of a woman's Spring season is learning how to wield the Sword of the Spirit to fight against the lies of her enemy.

God's Mighty Weapons

God has made promises in His Word to silence every voice that comes against you. He provides mighty weapons that will destroy all the lies of the enemy.

"No weapon turned against you will succeed. You will silence every voice raised up to accuse you. These benefits are enjoyed by the servants of the Lord; their vindication will come from me. I the Lord have spoken" (Isaiah 54:17, NLT).

"We use God's mighty weapons, not worldly weapons, to knock down the strongholds of human reasoning, and to destroy false arguments" (2 Corinthians 10:4, NLT).

A Mighty Woman

My mother, Helen, was in another Spring season of her life. She was pregnant again with her twelfth child and was growing attached to the tiny new life growing inside her. She woke up one morning with pain and cramping in her stomach. Her instinct was to call her doctor because she saw signs of possibly losing her baby.

She said that the doctor ordered her to stay in bed for the remainder of her pregnancy, so she wouldn't lose her baby, me. My dad made a feeble attempt to encourage her by saying, "It's okay if you lose this one we have eleven others to love." It was my dad's way of trying to comfort and encourage her, but it had the opposite effect—she got angry. She was determined to follow the doctor's orders and stay in bed every day for the next four months. Thanks, Mom.

I'm so glad my mother listened to the advice of her doctor. He said, "Helen, if you want to keep this baby you have to rest." Just like my mother trusted the doctor's orders to rest and stay off her feet, we must trust when we do our part to follow God's Word that we will reap a fruitful harvest.

"Then Jesus said, God's kingdom is like a seed thrown on the field by a man who then goes to bed and forgets about it. The seed sprouts and grows–he has no idea how it happens. The earth does it all without his help; first a green stem of grass, then a bud, then the ripened grain. When the grain is fully formed, he reaps–harvest time" (Mark 4:26-29, MSG)!

My mother told me that it was always her desire to have many children and she knew that a big family was God's purpose for her life.

I now realize, at the age of fifty-eight, that my mother had many of the qualities mentioned in the book of Proverbs. She was an amazing woman of determination and had a strong faith in God.

Just the fact that she gave birth to thirteen children makes her a mighty woman of God.

She was beautiful to look at and was easy to talk to. All the neighborhood kids loved spending time at our house because she was laid back, easy-going, and kind. She would sit at our kitchen table for hours with me and my friends and they would talk to her about all their problems. If they wanted to stay for dinner, no problem, just open another can of beans. She always had an open-door policy; everyone was welcome.

I was very fortunate that my mom was a stay-at-home mom. She was always there for her children because she didn't have to work outside of the home. But believe me, she had a twenty-four/seven, round-the-clock job. I'm sure her mansion in heaven is splendid. A friend once told me that she probably lives in a small condominium in heaven. I said, "Why do you think my amazing mother got awarded such a small place to live?" She said, "So none of you kids can move back in with her—don't you think she deserves some peace and quiet?" I thought that made good sense.

My mother was born in 1917 during World War 1 and was a young woman during the Great Depression. At some point during her childhood, her father decided to leave her mother to raise five children alone. She grew up watching her mother struggle to take care of her family. Her mother cleaned houses for a living and my mother remembers eating a lot of cabbage to survive in her growing up years. She started off in this life with very little but ended up being a very fruitful mother of thirteen children and many grandchildren.

She experienced many Winter seasons in her life, but she always stayed faithful to her belief in God and to her family. She struggled through raising thirteen children and had many insecurities in her life. Since she was raised in the Catholic Church, it was looked down upon to be pregnant out of wedlock. She carried a guilty conscience for most of her adult life because of her first pregnancy. She thought God could never forgive her because her mother said she wasn't worthy of a legitimate wedding. She believed those lies of the enemy for many years.

But when she turned sixty-two years old, she experienced a new beginning in her life. She was constantly worried about her kids, but one day her daughter, Carol, came home and told her that she finally understood that Jesus loved her. Carol shared the good news of the gospel with our mother. She said, "Mom, God loves you so much and He wants to have a personal relationship with you." Mom decided to talk to God that day and said, "God, I've had a fear of you my entire life and have tried to serve you to the best of my ability. My kids are telling me that you love me and want to forgive me for all my sins. Jesus, I want to know about your love, too."

God answered her prayers and Jesus made a home in her heart. For the first time in her life, she felt loved. She was overwhelmed by the indescribable joy that would bubble up on the inside of her. She would laugh and giggle for no other reason than her newfound relationship with God. She fell deeply in love with Jesus and wanted to spend hours alone with Him. My dad saw such a dramatic change in her after her supernatural encounter with God, he thought she was having an affair with another man.

"Anyone who believes in Me may come and drink! For the Scriptures declare, Rivers of living water will flow from his heart" (John 7:38, NLT).

My Sisters Know How to Fight

My father was a Golden Gloves boxing champion and very passionate about the sport. I can remember going with him to watch boxing matches when I was in the fourth grade. He was the referee at the Sacramento Memorial Auditorium. I'm not sure if it was his turn to babysit me, but for some reason, I was sitting in the front row of the boxing ring watching the fight. I didn't think there was anything strange about seeing my dad do his job. I thought it was exciting to observe the fighters as they danced around the ring and punched each other. From time to time I would get a little bit of blood splattered on me because I was sitting so close to them. At the end of the fight, the best man would win a prize!

My dad brought boxing gloves home and taught me and my sisters how to defend ourselves. I'm glad he showed his daughters how to wear boxing gloves, block and protect our faces, bob, and weave, and throw some punches. Those were our first lessons in conflict resolution. My dad thought it was important to teach his girls how to fight. Your heavenly Father wants to teach you how to fight and stand up for yourself, too. People think women don't know how to fight, but just watch us if someone says something negative about our kids; then you'll see a good fight. Trust me, I grew up with nine sisters—don't tell me women don't know how to fight!

"The apostle Paul teaches us how to fight the good fight of faith in the book of Timothy. He instructed Timothy, his son in the faith, how to fight and how to win. A good fight is only a fight that you win" (1 Timothy 6:12).

Women of Warfare Prepare

"It's important for women to be prepared for a fight every day because the devil has a strategic plan to devour us" (1 Peter 5:8).

Ephesians 6:10 says we should be strong in the Lord and the power of his might. Highly trained warriors constantly strengthen themselves for a possible attack. They know fighting is part of life and are not caught unaware. The Apostle Paul gives us the example of the toughened Roman soldier and how he prepared for the battles he would encounter. He encouraged the church in the book of Ephesians to imitate these soldiers and arm themselves with the full armor of God, so they would be empowered to stand against the wiles of the devil. (Ephesians 6:11-12)

The Holy Spirit Will Come Upon You

Ladies, if we're going to stay strong in our Spring season we'll have to strengthen ourselves with God's power. How do we stay strong in the Lord and the power of His might? Acts 1:8 says when the Holy Spirit comes upon us, He will give us the power we need to stay strong. We get strength when we're filled with the Holy Spirit. His supernatural presence comes into our lives when we praise and thank Him for everything.

"Speaking to one another with psalms, hymns, and songs from the Spirit. Sing and make music from your heart to the Lord, always giving thanks to God the Father for everything, in the name of our Lord Jesus Christ" (Ephesians 5:19b–20, NIV).

You may be asking yourself, "How much power is in a little song?" One day, Paul and Silas were minding their own business on their way to a prayer meeting and they met a girl who was possessed with a spirit of divination (demon). Every day while they walked to their prayer meeting, she followed Paul and Silas and yelled, "These men are servants of the most-high God." Paul got fed up with her daily antics. He was really getting annoyed and he commanded the evil spirit to come out of her in the Name of Jesus. She was instantly set free from the demonic spirit that was harassing them.

The girl's employer didn't appreciate Paul and Silas's good deed because he was making a lot of money from her gift of divination. Paul and Silas were beaten and thrown in jail.

I don't know about you, but if I was beaten and thrown in jail for helping someone get delivered from an evil spirit, singing and praising God is not the first thing I would do. When the devil beats up on me, my first response is usually to throw myself a pity party. I might cry and ask God, "How could this happen to me?" But

Paul and Silas knew the power of praise and the explosive effects it has on the demonic world.

"Around midnight Paul and Silas were praying and singing hymns to God, and the other prisoners were listening. Suddenly, there was a massive earthquake, and the prison was shaken to its foundation... and the chains of every prisoner fell off" (Acts 16:25-26, NLT).

Power in Praise

There is power in praise. Praying and singing releases the power of the Holy Spirit in our lives. Praising God breaks the spiritual chains that have kept us imprisoned. Singing and making melody in your heart will set you free from every kind of spiritual bondage and set you free from the prison of the enemy's lies.

Prayer: "Lord, I thank You and praise You for all You are doing in my life. I ask You to fill me with the power of the Holy Spirit as I praise You and thank You for setting me free from the lies of the enemy."

Do you often feel overcome and defeated by the lies of the enemy? You're in good company—most women experience the same kind of warfare from time to time. God is calling you to be a mighty woman by using the weapon of praise to break free from every demonic prison.

One of the weapons the enemy has used to intimidate me over and over is the spirit of fear. I've been knocked down many times as he aimed his fiery darts at me and whispered his lies in my ear. But I've learned, after years of fighting this opponent, to recognize his methods and strategies to keep me down. I stood and fought as I got tired of the spirit of fear keeping me from doing God's will.

Power, Love and a Sound Mind

The devil would like nothing better than to keep us in a perpetual state of fear, but God has given us everything we need to overcome every fear or spirit of intimidation that would try to keep us from standing strong. Ephesians 6:13 says, "So use every piece of God's armor to resist the enemy whenever he attacks, and when it is all over, you will still be standing up." Ephesians says if we wear God's armor we can stand against all the strategies, tricks, schemes, and devices of the enemy.

I began to understand that fear is a spirit and not part of God's perfect plan for my life. I combined faith with the Word of God to overcome the enemy's plan and his tactics. Second Timothy 1:7 says, "For God has not given us a spirit of fear, but of power and of love and a sound mind."

I declared, "I have His power and His might! He loves me and there is no fear in His love." When I place the helmet of salvation on my mind, I have the supernatural ability to think His thoughts. (Ephesians 6:17) The Holy Spirit gives us the power to have a godly thought life. He gives us His power over obsessive thoughts—which includes disciplined thought patterns, the ability to understand, and to make the right decisions, and self-discipline.

"So letting your sinful nature control your mind leads to death. But letting the Spirit control your mind leads to life and peace" (Romans 8:6, NLT).

Fear still tries to attack me, but I am confident and certain that the Holy Spirit can overcome any demon that tries to knock me out. I give thanks to God every day for saving me and giving me the ability to think clearly.

What happens when God gives you His love and power? It means you have His authority to cast out the spirit of fear… or any other harassing spirit. You can be free because the Holy Spirit lives on the inside of you. You can be delivered and set free from negative thoughts that try to paralyze you. Remember what the Lord told Zechariah in Zechariah 4:6? "It's not by might, nor by power, but by my Spirit says the Lord."

I've noticed that some of the best fighters are single moms. I so admire their fighting ability. I've observed how the enemy tries to take advantage of them by attacking them in their thought lives. He tries everything in his power to knock them out, but he is unable to win because they are standing on the Word of God and have put their trust in Him. They know how to get full of the power of the Holy Spirit and arm themselves with every weapon God has supplied for them. They wear the Armor of God. They know the Word of God. They are the spiritual prizefighters of this age.

Karen's Story

Karen didn't have the benefits of a stable childhood and she knew, as a young girl, that she needed to run away from her mother and her mother's boyfriend. If she and her sister were going to have a chance at happiness they would have to follow through with their plans to escape her mother's shakey lifestyle. I believe as you read her story you will be inspired to hear God's voice and be strengthened in your relationship with Him. Karen's story…

My parents were divorced when I was eight years old and my sister was six. Within a year, mom had a new boyfriend, Jesse, and with him came the party lifestyle. The year was 1964 and marijuana and LSD were making their way onto the party scene in the Bay Area (California).

Because of the free spirit attitude of my mom and Jesse, there was never regular work, or a regular house, or a regular school, just regular parties wherever we were. We lived in Mill Valley, Sausalito, San Francisco, San Leandro, Los Gatos, and Felton. And we went to school in all but one of those cities. When we didn't have our own place, we lived with my grandmother in Los Gatos, where I went to junior high school and survived more tumultuous years.

In 1968 my dad remarried. Then we started traveling by bus, during school vacations, by ourselves, to visit him and our new stepmom, Sherry. They lived on a ranch in Nevada with six horses! We loved horses and were so happy we could now learn to ride. By 1969, my dad and Sherry wanted us to come live with them. From our point of view, they had a regular home, regular jobs (she was a high school English teacher), regular cars that ran well, clothes that we got at K-Mart instead the thrift store, and a ranch with horses. We jumped at the chance to go live with them. We were so tired of the party scene! We were only twelve and ten years old and had no say, so we made the decision by ourselves. We started packing our stuff quietly and discreetly and hiding the boxes. In August 1969, while mom was in the shower, my dad and Sherry picked us up and we left California.

I started my freshman year of high school where Sherry taught English. My first real best friend, also Sherry's, was a Christian, and I met many of her Christian friends. One of the boys started to like me and asked me to go steady; I was thrilled! So, I started going to church or to youth meetings when I could—we lived twenty miles out of town—just to be with Joe, my boyfriend.

On April 12th, 1970, I told my parents that I wanted to go to church. It was there I prayed for Jesus to come into my heart. I didn't understand why Joe and the others were so happy for me, but soon I knew that I had met Jesus and that He was my Savior. I asked my dad for a Bible and he gave me his old one which I read from cover to cover during those years of high school even though I didn't understand anything that I was reading.

After Joe graduated, we broke up, so I didn't go into town to go to church very often anymore. But I continued to pray and read my Bible and every Summer saved enough money to pay my way to Christian Camp. That camp was my only church throughout my high school years.

I married my high school sweetheart from my senior year after he got saved, too. And the church in which we were married became my home church. They fed me, nurtured me, and supported me through thick and thin. By July 30, 1979, I was twenty-three years old, I had a four-year-old son, was four months pregnant with my second son, was unemployed, lost my stepmother, Sherry, in an automobile accident, and I was divorced.

I felt like God had deserted me. Where was He? I was afraid for myself and my children.

For the better part of the next few years, I learned that I was very self-centered and was truly helpless, despite how independent and self-sufficient I had believed myself to be. I could not do anything for myself. I did not have a job or job skills, and what sewing I did, took all my effort. I could not manage my money or even keep my house clean.

During these trials and troubles, I continued my habit of reading the Bible. And at this time in my life, I made it to Isaiah 54. The first three verses hit me when I started reading.

"Fear not; you will no longer live in shame. Don't be afraid; there is no more disgrace for you. You will no longer remember the shame of your youth and the sorrows of widowhood. For your Creator will be your husband; the Lord of Heaven's Armies is his name! He is your Redeemer, the Holy One of Israel, the God of all the earth. For the Lord has called you back from your grief—as though you were a young wife abandoned by her husband, says your God" (Isaiah 54:4-6, NLT).

Those two words, "fear not," literally jumped off the page at me when I read them that fateful day. The words seemed to come alive. The whole passage was like that and I knew that God was speaking to me personally about my situation. I started to cry. The first thing He wanted me to know was not to be afraid of whatever may happen. I believe God spoke those Words to me personally telling me that He was my husband. So, I began the journey of a lifetime: to find my security in God, my true and faithful husband.

Much of my fear was about how we would live, eat, and pay our bills. Without income, what was I going to do? God allowed me to be totally alone to lure me to Him. I *had* to get to know Him because I had no other logical, practical choice. I *had* to learn to depend on Him alone. I learned to pray for food, milk, and gas. I prayed for my power bill and my phone bill to be paid. I took in sewing, or decorated cakes, using my talents. I learned that paying my tithe was more important than any bill or need I had. If I was going to depend on God, then I needed to put my money where my mouth was and pay my tithe first. Even if I did just a two-dollar job of sewing, I gave twenty cents to the church.

I learned how to listen to God's Word, both in church and at home. I learned how to *act* on His Word and start thinking of others more than myself. I learned that these times really were for a small moment and God had not really forsaken me. I learned to stand on my own two feet as God strengthened my character and showed me that He always had bigger plans for me. And in the process, He took away all shame, regrets, and fear. I praise Him because He set me free!

Karen's inspirational life story is written in her book, *Romance with the Master,* which includes a small group workbook. She has trained herself to live a godly life and reaps the benefits of total dependence on God.

Win the Prize

Do you like prizes? Everyone wants to win a prize. I've seen people do the craziest things, to win one. You've seen them on the popular reality television shows. They leave their families for long periods of time to live with strangers. They deprive themselves of food and the daily comforts of home. They do terrible things to their bodies, just to win a prize that's not going to last.

"The Apostle Paul encouraged Timothy to discipline himself to fulfill the vision that God had given him: "Train yourself to live a godly life. Training the body helps a little, but godly living helps in every way" (1 Timothy 4:7-8).

The word 'training' implies athletic discipline—to vigorously exercise, train, and practice for proficiency. Without discipline, a vision will never be fulfilled. An athlete disciplines herself so that she may be able to perform her best in the competition. Your victory can only be reached through discipline and hard work. If we want to win the prize that will have long-lasting benefits, we must train ourselves the same way the Olympic winner trains herself to win the gold medal. As followers of Christ, the Apostle Paul encourages us to press toward our heavenly reward like the athlete that wins the race.

"I press on to reach the end of the race and receive the heavenly prize for which God through Christ Jesus is calling us" (Philippians 3:14, NLT).

God has called you to become more and more like Jesus because He has created you for a special purpose. And one of the ways to reach that calling is to be trained to fulfill the good works He has prepared for you.

"For we are His workmanship, [His own masterwork, a work of art], created in Christ Jesus [reborn from above—spiritually transformed, renewed, ready to be used] for good works, which God prepared [for us] beforehand [taking paths which He set], so that we would walk in them [living the good life which He prearranged and made ready for us]" (Ephesians 2:10, AMP).

During the 2016 Rio Olympics, Katie Ledecky won four gold medals in the freestyle swimming meets. She is a young woman who trained herself since she was six-years-old to be the best of the best, she totally dedicated herself to winning the prize. We can learn from her dedication to the sport on how to discipline ourselves to win the ultimate, eternal prize.

Most of us can't spend the amount of time and effort that an Olympic athlete invests into winning four gold medals, but the Apostle Paul is saying we need to be like her in pursuing our heavenly reward. He said if we train ourselves to live a godly life we can be successful in every area of our lives.

The rewards of discipline are great and there is a confidence that comes when we know we're training ourselves for a heavenly reward. There is a long-term sense of meaning, purpose, and direction to life. There is a freedom from the chaos and consequences of inaction or wrong actions.

"Don't you realize that in a race everyone runs, but only one person gets the prize? So, run to win! All athletes are disciplined in their training. They do it to win a prize that will fade away, but we do it for an eternal prize. So, I run with purpose in every step. I am not just shadowboxing. I discipline my body like an athlete, training it to do what it should. Otherwise, I fear that after preaching to others I myself might be disqualified" (1 Corinthians 9:24-27, NLT).

Finally, there's the reward in the ability to rest in knowing God is working in the spiritual part of your life. As we press on to know Him, He will respond to us and give us new strategies and routines to win the prize that's going to last forever.

Spring is a time with the purpose to plan and to plant. Because what you sow in the Spring will determine your harvest. Sow well, and you will reap and enjoy a good harvest. It's a sacrifice, and you have to part with your seed for a short time, but ultimately it comes back to you in multiplied measure.

A Time to Speak

"Ask the Lord for rain in the springtime; it is the Lord who sends the thunderstorms. He gives showers of rain to all people, and plants of the field to everyone" (Zechariah 10:1, NIV).

Take some time to speak God's Word over your Spring season and ask Him to water what you've planted. Jesus taught us to ask Him for the things we need. In Matthew 21:22 He told the disciples whatever things you ask for in prayer, believing, you will receive.

- I choose to plant seeds of love and righteousness today–Hosea 10:12; 1 Corinthians 13:4-8
- I will be a 'doer' of God's Word–James 1:22
- I will build my house with wisdom–Proverbs 14:1
- I believe God is working in me to do His will–Philippians 2:12-13
- He will direct my path as I seek Him–Proverbs 3:6
- He has given me every weapon to overcome my enemies–He trains me to fight–Ephesians 6:13
- I am strong in the Lord and the power of His might–Ephesians 6:10
    - Praising the Lord releases His power–Acts 16:25-26
    - He's given me power, love, and a sound mind–2 Timothy 1:7

Discussion Questions

Open Up: How can planting seeds of God's Word help your future harvest?

Share Scriptures: Let different members/friends share a verse or idea from this chapter that impacted them personally. What does it mean for you?

Talk It Over: How do our lives stay fresh and green? What are some ways a wise woman can build her house?

Pray Together: Pray for each other to listen to God's voice and use the Sword of the Spirit in a spiritual fight.

Prayer for the Spring Season:

Thank You, Lord, for helping me to be a woman of action and a 'doer' of Your Word. I want to plant seeds of righteousness into the soil of my life. As I spend time with You and walk in Your ways, please guide me every day. AMEN!

4
SUMMER AND THE KINGDOM OF GOD

Traditionally, for most of us, Summer is a time for vacations and relaxing. The heat causes us to retreat and look for cover, shade and rest. It's interesting to hear the stories of women who have a favorite season. Some enjoy the Fall season because of the beautiful harvest colors it provides and the good memories of the Thanksgiving holiday. I've always looked forward to Thanksgiving because turkey, stuffing, sweet potatoes, cranberry sauce and pumpkin pie are my favorite dishes of the year. Other women have good feelings from their great Summers filled with beach trips and warm, sunny weather. For those women who are teachers—they look forward to long Summer vacations and spending quality time with their friends and families.

In the early days of my life, my teenage friends and I would be so excited about Summer break—school was closed, and the community pool was open. We spent many days hitchhiking to the beach and enjoying our carefree lives. What were we thinking? We weren't old enough to know about all the possible dangers that could happen to four pretty, teenage girls hitchhiking to Santa Cruz. We were only thinking of the fun and good time we were going to have with our friends.

Later in life, I couldn't wait for my sons to finish the school year, so my husband and I could take them to the Hawaiian beaches to play in the ocean. Those special times can be awesome, and we need to rest, relax, and have fun, but is that the primary purpose God intends for our spiritual Summers—or is there something more important to discover?

In this chapter, we will see the connection Jesus makes between the Summer season and the acceleration of God's kingdom in our lives. He teaches us how to look for signs of growth in the Summer.

"Look at the fig tree, and all the trees. When they are already <u>budding</u>, you see and know for yourselves that <u>Summer</u> is near. So, you also, when you see these things happening, know that the <u>Kingdom of God is near</u>" (Luke 21:30-31, NKJV).

It's recorded in the book of Romans that the Kingdom of God is not meat or drink, but it's about right living, the peace of God and the joy of the Lord. A woman who is experiencing a Summer season may be enjoying the benefits of the seeds of love that were planted in her Spring season. Many women learn the secret of growing in their relationship with God in the Summer and they can see dramatic changes take place in their hearts as they believe what God says about them in His Word.

Jesus said unless you and I have an ongoing relationship with Him we won't be able to produce any lasting fruit. He wants to give you a vivid picture of the success you can enjoy when you're connected to Him.

"Take care to live in me and let me live in you. For a branch can't produce fruit when severed from the vine. Nor can you be fruitful apart from me. Yes, I am the Vine; you are the branches. Whoever lives in me and I in him shall produce a large crop of fruit. For apart from me you can't do a thing. But if you stay in me and obey my commands, you may ask any request you like, and it will be granted! My true disciples produce bountiful harvests. This brings great glory to my Father" (John 15:4-5, 7-8, TLB).

As you read the Words of Jesus, it's possible that you might see yourself as the unproductive branch and wonder why you haven't seen more fruit in your life. So many times, in my walk with the Lord, I've tried to solve my own problems without Him and I've spent sleepless nights, trusting in my own abilities to make my life fruitful. But time and time again, when I don't trust in Jesus and stay connected to Him—things don't turn out so good. I'm determined to stay vitally connected to Him because I know it's the only way that I can bear any lasting fruit. You and I can produce a bountiful harvest if we obey the words of Jesus.

As you continue reading this chapter, you will meet some women who went through some stormy weather in their lives, but they decided to put their trust in God and learned how to grow and be successful even in the hottest time of their Summer season.

The Kingdom of God is Near

In the Summer of 1970, my father was promoted at his job and moved our family from Sacramento to Sunnyvale, California. There were still six of his thirteen children living under his roof. On our way to our new home in Sunnyvale, he drove through the streets of San Francisco to show us where He would be working near Market Street. We wanted to know if we were going to see any hippies there, otherwise known as flower children. A hippie is a young person, rejecting conventional society and advocating love, peace, and simple idealistic values. During the late sixties and early seventies, young people gathered in San Francisco and the surrounding cities during the Summer of Love.

My siblings and I knew that all hippies lived in San Francisco because we heard Scott McKenzie's song on the radio, *Are you going to San Francisco?*

> If you're going to San Francisco
> Be sure to wear some flowers in your hair
> If you're going to San Francisco
> You're gonna meet some gentle people there

> For those who come to San Francisco
> Summertime will be a love-in there
> In the streets of San Francisco
> Gentle people with flowers in their hair
>
> All across the nation
> Such a strange vibration
> People in motion
> There's a whole generation
> With a new explanation
> People in motion
> People in motion
>
> For those who come to San Francisco
> Be sure to wear some flowers in your hair
> If you come to San Francisco
> Summertime will be a love-in there
>
> If you come to San Francisco
> Summertime will be a love-in there

Songwriters: John Edmund Andrew Phillips

San Francisco lyrics © Universal Music Publishing Group

    We were so excited when we met some flower children with their long, stringy hair and tie-dyed clothes. My teenage siblings liked their hip look—grew long hair and transformed themselves into hippies overnight. I followed their example and grew my hair long, too.

    It was a new season for my family in the city of Sunnyvale. I was nervous about going into the sixth-grade where I met a whole group of new friends. It was easy for me to assimilate into my new school because I was good at sports and not too shy. I then went to Junior High School and met some pre-teens who were experimenting with marijuana and other illegal drugs. Kids at that age want so much to be liked and accepted by their peers, they'll do just about anything to fit in with their friends.

My new friends were a part of this *"new generation from across the nation"* that Scott McKenzie sang about. I thought it was exciting to smoke pot with my new friends because it helped me to be accepted by them. I wanted to feel like I was a part of their group, so I followed their example.

Some of my siblings became a part of this new generation—they believed the lie that drugs and free love would bring them the fulfillment they were longing for in their lives. These so-called *gentle people* had a major impact on my family. You can imagine what that did to my seriously Catholic parents who were working hard to keep all their children on the straight and narrow road.

During the early seventies, hundreds of hippies and flower children were part of this new generation who were influenced by the culture of drugs, sex, and rock 'n roll music. There was definitely *a strange vibration and a generation with a new explanation* influencing my family.

At the same time, God was on the move and had plans to invade this new generation of hippies with His love. Some called what was happening to young people all over the world, *The Jesus Movement*. This was a time in history when God lavishly poured out His Holy Spirit on thousands of young people, and they were surrendering their hearts to Jesus.

The prophet Joel predicted the outpouring of the Holy Spirit centuries ago:

"In the last days, God says, I will pour out my Spirit upon all people, your sons and daughters will prophesy. Your young men will see visions, and your old men dream dreams. In those days I will pour out my Spirit even on my servants—men and women alike—and they will prophesy" (Acts 2:16-18. NLT).

The *Jesus Movement* was an Evangelical Christian movement beginning on the West Coast of the United States in the late 1960s and early 1970s and spreading primarily throughout North America, Europe, and Central America, before subsiding by the late 1980s. Members of the movement were called *Jesus People*, or *Jesus Freaks*.

A New Season

My sister, Carol, recently told me she felt so sad and lonely when she was fourteen years old, that she began drinking and taking drugs with her Catholic girlfriends—wanting so much to be accepted. She thought that drinking and drugs could fill the sad, depressed hole in her heart. At that point in her life, it was the worst thing in the world not to have a boyfriend—which for sure meant something must be terribly wrong with her. She was filled with shame—almost a desperate search for acceptance—but no person could ever fill that emptiness.

One day, Carol was visiting with her teenage friend, Monica, at her home. Monica's brother, a holiness preacher, talked to them about the love of Jesus and told them they needed to be "saved." He told them, Jesus came to forgive every one of their sins and desired to make their lives brand new. But, he said, "you must repent (change your mind and turn your life around—walk in a different direction.)" He also shared that it wasn't enough just to know about Jesus, but he wanted them to understand they could have a relationship with Him.

"Because of his kindness, you have been saved through trusting Christ. And even trusting is not of yourselves; it too is a gift from God. Salvation is not a reward for the good we have done, so none of us can take any credit for it" (Ephesians 2:8-9, TLB).

Carol and Monica knew what he said was true, but they decided they would wait a year because they weren't quite ready to get "saved."

A few months after our family moved from Sacramento to Sunnyvale, Carol's teenage world was turned upside down. She had left all her childhood support system behind and moved into a new season of her life. She missed all her multicultural friends who loved listening to Soul and Motown music. She was devastated and depressed, trying to find new friends in her new school—only to find hippies who loved smoking dope and listening to Acid Rock music. Navigating her last year of high school alone was earth-shattering, but she kept thinking about the conversation she had with Monica's brother—YOU NEED TO BE SAVED! Her thoughts kept turning to God—She was thinking about Him and writing songs about Him—even while she continued to take drugs with her new friends.

"If you openly declare that Jesus is Lord, and believe in your heart that God raised Him from the dead, you will be saved. For it is by believing in your heart that you are made right with God, and it is by openly declaring your faith that you are saved" (Romans 10:9-10, NLT).

Carol was so happy when she finally made some friends at her new school who were into art and music. One day they invited her to an art show and as she walked into the show, she could hear a band singing about Jesus and God. It then dawned on her that her new friends must be Christians, so she walked a little slower, away from her friends, because she didn't want people to think she was with them.

On the ride home, her friend asked her if she wanted to go to church the next morning. She didn't know how to say "no," so she reluctantly said "yes," hoping her friend would forget about the invitation. But to her dismay, her friend arrived on her front doorstep, bright and early, the next morning to take her to church. Little did her friend know that Carol was searching for a way out of her life of sadness, loneliness, and drugs.

I walked into Peninsula Bible church and I remember there was singing and a sermon. I don't remember what was sung or what was preached. I only remember that it was like a lightbulb moment and all the sudden I thought "oh, that's who Jesus is." I knew I was born again—just like Monica's brother said the previous year.

On the ride home from church that day, Central Expressway was literally lined with Spring flowers, and I was so filled with joy that my face ached from smiling. I went home and fell at my mother's feet and cried, "Mom, you need to be saved and ask Jesus into your heart."

Carol simply believed what the preacher said that morning and asked Jesus to forgive her of all her past sins. Her new life started, and she became born again. Well, as you can imagine, that caused quite a ruckus in the very seriously Catholic family— Catholic schools, and mandatory church every Sunday. She remembers being taught about Jesus, but she didn't know she could have a life-changing relationship with Him.

When Carol accepted Jesus into her heart—being born again was life-transforming. She became a new person and was renewed by the Holy Spirit! She wanted to share with everyone she met about the amazing things that were happening in her life because she was happier than she had ever been before.

"Therefore, if anyone is in Christ, he is a new creation; old things have passed away; behold, all things have become new" (2 Corinthians 5:17 (NKJV)

Carol was part of this *new generation with a new explanation,* but it wasn't about sex, drugs and rock 'n' roll. Instead of inviting all her teenage friends over to her house for beer parties, her new Christian friends were on a quest to search the Scriptures to understand what it meant to be renewed by the Holy Spirit. They now wanted to pray and study their Bibles.

Well, our parents didn't totally comprehend the new things taking place in her life, but you can believe they enjoyed seeing the positive changes taking place before their very eyes.

You Need the Holy Spirit

Jesus said that His true followers produce a bountiful harvest and the large crop of fruit, the fruit of the Holy Spirit—the fruits of love, joy, peace, patience, kindness, goodness, faithfulness, gentleness and self-control—these are evident when we're in a continual relationship with Him.

Jesus used colorful parables to teach his disciples about the Kingdom of God. Many verses in the Bible draw our attention to fruitful trees that bear all kinds of luscious fruit. He describes a branch that bears delicious fruit when it's vitally connected to a vine. He said we are the branches and He is the Vine. In other Words, when we continually spend quality time with Him and faithfully follow what He says we become like Him and produce a bountiful harvest.

I've noticed that I'm strongly influenced by the women I allow to speak into my life. I had one friend that I will call "Sally." She was always negative about everything that was happening in her life; I can't remember one positive remark about anything or anyone. I always felt depressed and like a heavy load of garbage was hanging on me when I would visit with her. My husband could see that I behaved differently when I spent time with her and on one occasion he asked me, "were you with Sally today?" I was surprised by his question and said, "how did you know?" He said, "I can see she her negativity has affected you—you seem depressed and down."

On the other hand, women who are full of the Holy Spirit have a positive effect on me. When I am with people who are upbeat and connected to Jesus, I'm full of life—I feel peaceful and happy. Their encouraging demeanor builds me up instead of tearing me down.

Jesus said you will know them by their fruit.

"You will know them by their fruits. Do men gather grapes from thornbushes or figs from thistles? Even so, every good tree bears good fruit, but a bad tree bears bad fruit. A good tree cannot bear bad fruit, nor can a bad tree bear good fruit. Every tree that does not bear good fruit is cut down and thrown into the fire. Therefore, by their fruits, you will know them" (Matthew 7:16-20, NKJV).

I prayed with a young lady the other day and she listed the many fears and anxieties she was facing daily. I reminded her that Jesus loves her so much and she was specifically chosen to bear an abundance of fruit. (John 15:16)

We don't have to live our lives filled with fear and anxiety because He's made some amazing promises to women who stay connected to Him. One of the ways we experience supernatural peace–the God-kind of peace–is by talking to Him about everything.

"Do not be anxious or worried about anything, but in everything [every circumstance and situation] by prayer and petition with thanksgiving, continue to make your [specific] requests known to God. And the peace of God [that peace that reassures the heart, that peace] which transcends all understanding [that peace which] stands guard over your hearts and your minds in Christ Jesus [is yours]" (Philippians 4:6-7, AMP).

It's impossible to live a life that is full of love, joy, and peace apart from Jesus, but when we're communing with Him and doing what He says, we will produce large crops of fruit. Anytime we allow Him to control our lives, He will bring about the qualities of the Holy Spirit spoken of in the book of Galatians.

"But when the Holy Spirit controls our lives he will produce this kind of fruit in us; love, joy, peace, patience, kindness, goodness, faithfulness, gentleness and self-control" (Galatians 5:22-23, TLB).

The Love of God is Near

One night while I was trying to sleep, I was awakened at one o'clock by someone making a strange noise. This unusual sound was coming through the bedroom wall. My sister, Carol's bedroom was on the other side. She was crying and praying for all of us sinners who slept in the adjacent bedroom. As I listened to her talking to God, I found out my entire family was a bunch of sinners; me, my sisters and brothers were the sinners who needed saving. She cried out to God, "Lord, please save Lisa, Kathy, Danny, Judy, Joanne, Tommy, Martha, Pat, Dicky, Susan, Sandra, Connie, Mom, and Dad!" She kept praying, "I don't want them to go to hell, please save them."

Of course, she would know better than anyone else the kind of sinners we were, since we lived in the same house and she was a partner to our crimes. I got so mad, I thought, "What is her problem?" I yelled through the wall, "Shut up, I'm trying to sleep!" She didn't let up, night after night, she prayed and cried out—until most of us sinners repented of our sins and gave our hearts to the Lord, too. As you may or may not know, God answers the passionate prayers of the righteous! (James 5:16)

I soon became a brand-new person, too, just like my sister. My life was totally transformed by the love of Jesus from that time until now. My thought life began to change—I miraculously began to think loving thoughts about people—the way I talked, the way I behaved began to change, too. I wanted God to change my rebellious teenage ways and he answered my prayers. God was doing a spiritual work in my heart by the power of the Holy Spirit.

Women notice when other women get something new—new shoes, new phone, a new car or a new hairstyle. One day I went to get a manicure at the nail salon and I was talking to my manicurist about our lives. We talked about our husbands, our children's ages and where they attend school and, of course, we talked about our feelings. She said: "I've noticed there's something different about you, what is it? You seem happy every time I see you." I said "Do you really want to know why I'm happy? Because if you really want to know what's different about me, I'm going to tell you." She said, "whatever you have, I want it."

Now, I was honest with her and I told her the reason I was happy, was because I had met Jesus. He was the Person who made the difference in my life. I went on to tell her that I wasn't always happy, there were many times in my life when I was sad, but when I met Jesus, He gave me a new heart. I began to share His love with her—I said, "He will come into your heart, too, if you simply invite Him into your life and ask Him to forgive you of all of your past mistakes—He will make you brand new, too." She smiled at me and said, "I want Jesus to come into my heart and make me happy like you."

A few months after I invited Jesus into my life I was talking to my father. He was thrilled about the amazing changes that took place in my life because just a few weeks before that he was chasing me around the house with a belt for coming home late. He could see the dramatic impact Jesus made in me and he said, "Kathy, you're different than you used to be, and you've become a whole new person."

"But when the kindness and the love of God our Savior toward man appeared, not by works of righteousness which we have done, but according to His mercy He saved us, through the washing of regeneration and renewing of the Holy Spirit" (Titus 3:4-5, NKJV).

The New Kid on the Front Row

It was Easter Sunday morning, the choir director worked for months ahead of time to choose the perfect songs. She picked the ones that would inspire the church to believe that Jesus loved them. The choir and the musicians had practiced hundreds of hours—the big day was finally here. The church was decorated to look like Spring, the lighting on the platform was a warm lavender and created just the right mood. Three services were planned with the expectation of large crowds and my husband, David, gave an inspirational message about the *God of Miracles.* We made it through the first two services with flying colors and several visitors gave their hearts to the Lord that morning. All our hard work was paying off. There's nothing like seeing the lives of people transformed by the love of Jesus. The third worship service was in play, but who was the new kid who appeared on the front row of the choir? The worship leader said she never saw him at any rehearsals or in the first or second service. But there he was, front and center, waving his hands at his parents and making funny faces—he didn't know any of the Words to the songs.

I could totally relate to the kid on the front row—I didn't want to live in a fishbowl where I was expected to dress or act a certain way. I just wanted to be a part of God's house and enjoy the great things He was doing in my life. When my husband and I began dating, I learned that he was a rather intense person. I could see that he was very serious and loved Jesus with all his heart. One day he made an announcement to me, "if you want to date me, you have to eat, drink and sleep the ministry." I thought that was a weird statement coming from a boy who was just sixteen-years-old. If he was trying to woo me with his romantic words, he was failing miserably. I thought, who died and made him God? I answered him with the same intensity, "I love Jesus, too, but I'm not crazy! I'm a teenager and I want to have fun."

I knew the kind of person I was just a few months before I met Jesus. Every time I looked in the mirror I would see the scars on my face from the time I dove into the water at the Lexington Reservoir face first. It was on one of those Summer days that I hitched a ride up Highway 17. I was having a great time swimming and drinking with my friends, so I wasn't thinking clearly. I dove into the shallow water and when I stood up, my face was covered in blood. I looked like someone punched me in the face and beat the living daylights out of me. Every time I look in the mirror, I can still see scars on my upper lip and my forehead reminding me of that awful day.

During our engagement, my husband was hired to work at our church and wanted to be a full-time pastor. Being newly married to a minister made me feel like the new kid on the front row—God just placed me in the spotlight—and all His people were watching me. I was young and inexperienced in the ways of church dynamics. I was immediately expected to be a leader of women, teach Sunday school classes, pray for people in the hospital, counsel married couples, cook meals for shut-ins, administrate events for hundreds of people—I felt inadequate—I wasn't prepared to fulfill all the expectations that the congregation had for me. I didn't know the right words to say and I didn't know how to act as a pastor's wife.

I would compare myself to the female guest speakers that came to our church, who had a certain look and had a perfect appearance. These women were so gifted. They knew how to play the piano, the organ, had memorized hundreds of Scriptures, cooked gourmet meals, and had spotless houses. I would think to myself, "I can't dress like them, or speak with perfect diction like they do." I pretty much say what's on my mind and that's not always a good thing. But as I grew closer to Jesus—the Holy Spirit helped me with my insecurities and fears.

Sometimes I would focus on my past mistakes, but I remembered a story in the Bible when Jesus was teaching in the temple. The religious teachers brought a woman who was caught in the act of adultery to him. They wanted her to pay for her sins, but Jesus didn't accuse or condemn her for her mistakes. He lovingly forgave her and said, "go and sin no more" (John 8:1-15).

A New Person

Jesus didn't come to condemn you for your mistakes or to accuse you for not being perfect. Anyone who is in Christ is a new person—that means YOU! Jesus died on a cross to forgive you for all the old things of the past. If you stay stuck in the past, then you can't embrace the wonderful new things He has for your future.

I told you some of the stupid seasons of my life and God knows the secret sins I've committed over the years. When I started my new life with Jesus, I remember feeling condemned when I would think about diving face first into the Lexington dam—when I looked in the mirror I could see the scars on my face. But now, when I investigate the mirror, I see God's forgiveness, His love, and compassion. I see the new person He has created me to be.

All of us have scrapes, bruises, and scars from our past—Jesus came to give us a second, third, and fourth new beginning. The Bible says his mercies are new every morning—that means you can start fresh every day. Jesus has a wonderful plan for your life and He came to share His abundant blessings with you—a life filled with His love.

I love the way The Message translation explains how much Jesus loves us.

"This is how much God loved the world: He gave his Son, his one and only Son. And therefore: so that no one need be destroyed; by believing in Him, anyone can have a whole and lasting life. God didn't go to all the trouble of sending His Son merely to point an accusing finger, telling the world how bad it was. He came to help, to put the world right again" (John 3:16-17, MSG).

He Will Make All My Dreams Come True

My husband and I taught a five-week series at our church entitled "Let's Talk: Relationships." As I was studying the topic of love in I Corinthians 13, it dawned on me, I still have a long way to go. Even though I've been married thirty-five years and I've read about God's love for over forty years, I'm still learning how to play nice with others. Surely, by this time in my life, I should have a doctorate in the Language of Love, and loving others should just come automatically, right?

"Love is not puffed up, love does not behave rudely, does not seek its own, is not provoked, thinks no evil, does not rejoice in iniquity, but rejoices in the truth, bears all things, believes all things, hopes all things, endures all things. Love never fails" (1 Corinthians 13:4-8, KJV).

The more we live a life of love, and continue in a deep relationship with Jesus, the more He enables us to live our life His way. And the more we get to know God, we find out love is an action and not just romantic words in a song. I remember when I was dating my husband, I thought—I've finally met the man who is going to make all my dreams come true—it was all about me, me, me. I had the wrong idea about the meaning of love—especially God's kind of love. I discovered if I want to produce the fruit of the Holy Spirit, I would have to partner with God and give it my best effort.

"For this is how God loved the world, He gave His One and Only Son so that everyone who believes in Him will not perish but have eternal life" (John 3:16, NLT).

The Word love in this verse is 'agape' love and describes the selfless, unconditional love Jesus has for all of us. He said, I didn't come to be served, but I came to serve. He acted on our behalf. and He showed us how to love—He GAVE.

"Your attitude must be like My own, for I the Messiah, did not come to be served, but to serve, and to give My life a ransom for many" (Matthew 20:28, TLB).

Love is acting for another person's good. It's not just an *ooey-gooey* feeling of love that we see in romance movies, it's about our behavior—how we behave, how we act, how we serve. Our loving actions will determine how successful we are in our relationships. Our commitment to behave in a loving manner for someone else's good will produce the kind of family and church relationships we want to build.

A Sweet Aroma

I walked into Safeway the other day to do my grocery shopping and I was instantly met with the sweet smell of cinnamon rolls. The bakery had just finished cooking their world-famous buns. I wasn't thinking about them when I entered those glass doors, but that sweet-smelling aroma drew me to the back of the store. Do you know that you can create a sweet atmosphere around you when you're filled with His love? When you and I give ourselves sacrificially to others we are just like those sweet cinnamon rolls, we have a sweetness about us that is attractive.

"Imitate God in everything you do, because you are his dear children. Live a life filled with love, following the example of Christ. He loved us and offered himself as a sacrifice for us, a pleasing aroma to God. For this light within you produces only what is good and right and true" (Ephesians 5:1-4, 9, NLT).

When our lives are filled with his love, we act like God, we give ourselves to others—and that's not easy—it's hard work! Because we have the love of Jesus, we can produce a life of goodness and we can permeate this world with a sweet-smelling fragrance.

Sisters Dory and Jenny Pieters were single moms raising their five daughters together. I met them in 1975 at an all-night prayer meeting—they exuded the love of Jesus—always helping and providing for others. Not only were they running their own small business, working to provide for their families, but they faithfully led others in worship services, prayer meetings, spent countless hours counseling, teaching and mentoring the younger generation in our church for over forty years. I will forever be grateful to them for carrying the sweet love of Jesus to the hundreds of people in our church.

I've been drawn to Jesus many times because of the sweet aroma that came from the amazing women who lived exemplary lives. Dory and Jenny followed Jesus with all their hearts and fulfilled Ephesians 5 by their undying love for Him. They courageously sacrificed their lives, so others could live the blessed life.

SUMMER IS A TIME TO GROW

God has given you a dream and you have emerged from the Winter season. Because you have been diligent and proactive, your Spring seed is in the ground. Now, how do you direct your efforts in the Summer season? Women who are in a relationship with Jesus know the Kingdom of God is near because they are in daily intimate contact with Him.

"I planted and Apollos watered, but God made it grow. So, neither the one who plants nor the one who waters are important because only God makes it grow. We are God's coworkers" (1 Corinthians 3:6-9, GWT).

We only come into our season of blessing through a partnership with God. Notice the sequence in 1 Corinthians 3:6-9: plant, water, grow. Planting and watering our seeds is our part.

Growth is God's part. Paul is telling us: Don't wait for God to do it all. Do your part and God will bring an increase.

Working on our relationships will cost us something and offering ourselves to others is not always convenient. It means we must give of our time, our talent—it takes effort and hard work. The same is true in our relationship with God—we grow when we work with God.

"So that you may live a life worthy of the Lord and please Him in every way: bearing fruit in every good work, growing in the knowledge of God" (Colossians 1:6, NIV).

"This is a faithful saying, and these things I want you to affirm constantly, that those who have believed in God should be careful to maintain good works. These things are good and profitable to men" (Titus 3:8, NKJV).

In the natural, Summer brings the initial signs of the harvest and some first-fruits. A wise farmer sees this, and he gets to work because he knows that something good is near. Jesus said you will see things accelerating in your spiritual Summer and the newness of God's kingdom will be revealed to you. Rather than relax in the Summer, I believe we need to "make hay while the sun shines" because we are close to a rewarding season.

"A wise son harvests in the Summer" (Proverbs 10:5, CEB).

Water Makes You Grow

Have you ever lived in a tropical country that is hot and humid all year round? My husband and I were sent from our church to work as missionaries for a year in the Philippine Islands. We had to adjust to living in the hot and sticky weather—at times the humidity seemed unbearable. It caused us to overheat and we were constantly dripping with sweat. Our bodies were not accustomed to the muggy air, so we encountered some health risks.

Shortly after we arrived, my husband was doing some construction work outdoors and he became severely dehydrated. He got terribly sick because he wasn't drinking enough water. His muscles were cramping—he was experiencing low energy and feelings of dizziness and confusion.

In those days we didn't have Google to look up his medical condition. Luckily, we brought a medical book with us and were able to look up his unusual symptoms and realized he had heat exhaustion. We were able to remedy his problem quickly with salt tablets and tons of water.

One of the dangers of Summer is dehydration due to the warmer temperatures. Lawns and plants dry out more quickly in the heat, so they need a lot of water to stay fresh and green. The Word of God speaks of carefully nourishing that which has been planted. In every area of our lives, we need to apply the water of God's Word to accomplish a fruitful lifestyle. Just as it's true that our potted plants and flowers will wilt and die if we don't water them, the same applies to our spiritual lives.

"As the rain and the snow come down from heaven, and do not return to it without watering the earth and making it bud and flourish...so is my Word...It will not return to me empty, but it will accomplish what I desire and achieve the purpose for which I sent it" (Isaiah 55:1-11, NIV).

This verse likens God's Word to the rain and snow. Just as the rain and the snow water our plants and make them grow—God's Word waters us every time we read it, hear it and sing it. The Word of God saturates our thirsty souls and fulfills His purpose and causes us to flourish.

As I look at my neighborhood, some of the beautiful green plants and colorful flowers are wilting because of the four-year drought in California. The same is true for us when we are spiritually dry and suffer from a lack of refreshing from God's Word.

Sometimes we're not growing in our relationship with the Lord because we haven't taken the necessary time to replenish our spiritual gardens during the heat of our Summer season. We can refresh ourselves every day from God's never-ending fountain because it never runs dry.

"Those who believe Him discover that God is a fountain of truth. For this one—sent by God—speaks God's Words, for God's Spirit is upon him without measure or limit" (John 3:33-34, TLB).

Take All My Problems

My sister, Joanne, was telling me the story of the time she woke up to the sound of a flying airplane. She was shocked to find out that she was a passenger on a flight to San Jose, California. This wasn't a dream, it was more like a nightmare because the last thing she remembered was driving her car with her two-year-old son in the back seat. She was pulled over by a police officer due to her irregular driving. She had taken some pills to get high that day, but she couldn't remember what she took. The policeman told her she had two choices—she could go to jail or walk home. She agreed to the latter and attempted to walk home, but she passed out on the sidewalk. Her young son went up to a nearby house and knocked on the door. He told the lady who answered the door that his mommy was sick, and she needed help.

Joanne was like many young teenagers in the late 60s and early 70s who were experimenting with all kinds of illegal drugs. In her senior year of high school, she began to drink and went to a lot of parties. Shortly after enrolling in college, she married her first husband. He taught her how to enjoy different ways to get high. She and her husband were entangled with the wrong crowd and began experimenting with heroin; he became an addict and he struggles to this day.

Joanne got pregnant and they had a beautiful son together, but they didn't have a clue how to be good parents or how to make their marriage work. Unfortunately, after her son was born, their marriage ended in a divorce. She tried to raise her son alone with her limited knowledge and meager income, but she wasn't doing a very good job of it.

Her life went into a rapid decline after her divorce and she submerged herself into late-night parties—drinking, smoking marijuana, and popping pills. Her destructive lifestyle peaked with the use of heroin and at one point she remembers taking so many kinds of pills that she became temporarily blind. She was so messed up that she crashed her car and left it in an empty parking lot. She somehow found a phone and called a friend to come and pick her up.

During this horrific season of Joanne's life, she received many letters from her sister, encouraging her to turn her life over to Jesus. Every time she went to her mailbox, there was another letter from her mother or her sister. Joanne became increasingly annoyed as she opened the mailbox to find another letter filled with written prayers.

One of the letters from her mother said she had some great news to share and that she recently prayed to ask Jesus to live in her heart. She went on to explain that she had a talk with God and handed all her problems (meaning her thirteen children) over to Him. She encouraged Joanne that she should do the same and give all her problems to Jesus, too.

At the same time, Joanne was employed by the same company as our father and older brother. They were receiving phone calls from their co-workers who reported that Joanne was coming to work under the influence of drugs. Joanne's father and brother conspired to get her on the next flight to San Jose, hoping she would move back in with her parents and get her life straightened out.

When she arrived at the San Jose airport, her sisters were there to collect her and take her home. She was very angry that her family had forced her on the airplane and expected her to shape up. She left her parents' home the first chance she got and hitched a ride from a truck driver back to her friends in Sacramento.

After a few days of partying with her friends, she was filled with despair and the words of her mother kept playing in her mind, "Just turn all of your problems over to Jesus."

One day while Joanne was sitting at her desk at work she began to think clear thoughts and became very sad because of the way she had an endangered her son by her crazy behavior. She knew she needed help and was totally out of answers. She didn't know how to get free from her addictions, so she decided she was going to talk to God and ask Him for help. She prayed her first prayer and asked Jesus to take all her problems.

She immediately got on the phone to call her mother to tell her the good news. She said, "Mom, I'm coming home." Her mother said, "I've been waiting for your phone call because the Holy Spirit told me to expect a call from you."

She was in a spiritually broken, dry time of her life, but while she was staying with her parents, Joanne's sister shared how the love of Jesus was changing her life. Joanne believed that His love could do the same for her. She asked Jesus to come into her life and was miraculously delivered from her addictions. Joanne has been walking with the Lord for over forty years and continues to let the Holy Spirit work in her life.

"And we also thank God constantly for this, that when you received the Word of God, which you heard from us, you accepted it not as the Word of men but as what it really is, the Word of God, which is at work in you believers" (I Thessalonians 2:13, ESV).

The Planting of the Lord

As a new Christian, I soon realized I couldn't live this new, abundant life apart from my relationship with Jesus and the people of God. If I was going to continue to live my life for Him, I needed to be taught and encouraged—and watered—by other believers to stay rooted.

The deeper I allowed myself to be planted in God's house, the stronger I grew, the more stable and secure I became in Him. One of the many benefits of being planted in a great church is being built up by solid teachers.

"So then, just as you received Christ Jesus as Lord, continue to live your lives in Him, rooted and built up in Him, strengthened in the faith as you were taught and overflowing with thankfulness" (Colossians 2:6-7, NIV).

Psalm 92:11-15 says the person who is planted in His House shall flourish—even in their old age they will continue to be fruitful.

"The righteous man will flourish like the palm tree, He will grow like a cedar in Lebanon. Planted in the house of the Lord, they will flourish in the courts of our God. They will still yield fruit in old age; they shall be full of sap and very green, to declare that the Lord is upright; He is my rock, and there is no unrighteousness in Him" (Psalm 92:12-15, NIV).

Are you planted in His House? The only way a righteous woman can prosper, blossom, and thrive is when she is planted in the house of God. Just as a palm tree cannot flourish on its own, a righteous woman cannot move forward in her relationship with God without being planted in His house. Have you ever seen a palm tree in stormy weather? A palm tree can only survive in adverse weather because it's deeply rooted and fixed deeply in the soil.

Women are usually drawn into God's house because of one of the things listed in the book of Isaiah. I've seen them come to

God because of their broken hearts, addictions, sadness or depression. They might turn to Him because of a financial need, an emotional trauma, or possibly a betrayal by someone they love. Jesus has good news for women who are suffering and afflicted. He is anointed to help you no matter what terrible season you are living in or lived through. Even if you were born into a dysfunctional family and were neglected in your childhood, Jesus has the answer for every heartache and He can mend the broken pieces of your life.

"The Spirit of the Lord God is upon me, because the Lord has anointed Me to bring good news to the suffering and afflicted. He has sent Me to comfort the brokenhearted, to announce liberty to captives, and open the eyes of the blind; He has sent Me to tell those who mourn that the time of God's favor to them has come, and the day of His wrath to their enemies. To all who mourn in Israel you will give: beauty for ashes; joy instead of mourning; praise instead of heaviness. For God has planted them like strong and graceful oaks for His own glory" (Isaiah 61:1-4, TLB).

You may believe that your season is never going to change, and you'll always be stuck in pain, but you can be strong and healed because He proclaims freedom to the captives and releases prisoners from darkness… any kind of darkness. He comforts everyone who mourns. He will restore you to a place of joy and He will give you beauty for ashes.

God can touch you, heal you and set you free, but unless you allow Him to plant you, your freedom will be short-lived. If you let your roots grow deep, you will be like a well-watered tree of righteousness who always bear fruit.

"Blessed is the man who trusts in the Lord and whose trust is the Lord, for he will be like a tree planted by the water, that extends its roots by a stream and will not fear when the heat comes; but its leaves will be green, and it will not be anxious in a year of drought nor cease to yield fruit" (Jeremiah 17:7-8, NASB).

His Sunshine Makes You Grow

"But for you who obey me, my saving power will rise on you like the sun and bring healing like the sun's rays. You will be as free and happy as calves let out of a stall" (Malachi 4:2, GNT).

My husband and I have always been curious as to why we feel so good when we go to Hawaii. We love being in the sun because it revitalizes and refreshes us. An article we read about the sun highlighted all the advantages of sunlight, it's mood-lifting because it releases serotonin and makes you feel calm and focused. Without enough sun our bodies experience low levels of serotonin and that can cause feelings of depression. Five to fifteen minutes of sunlight a day give vitamin D-boosting benefits. Exposure to the sun's rays plays a role in bone health and many other healing properties according to www.Healthline.com.

You need a lot of sunshine to grow and be healthy. God's presence is like the natural sunshine and provides a multitude of benefits. Even as the natural sunlight affects your mood and emotional balance, God's spiritual sunlight will fill strengthen you, it will fill you with the joy, and bring healing to your life.

The Sunlight of His Presence

You can have the most beautiful, green plant, but if it doesn't get the nourishment of the sun, it will die. Even as a plant needs the natural sunlight, you must have the sunlight of His presence if you're going to grow in Him. The darker our world grows the more we need the sunlight of God's presence. That's why the Lord told Aaron and his sons to give this blessing to the people of Israel:

"May the Lord bless and protect you; may the Lord's face radiate with joy because of you; may he be gracious to you, show you his favor, and give you his peace. This is how Aaron and his sons shall call down my blessings upon the people of Israel; and I myself will personally bless them" (Numbers 6:24-27, TLB).

This world creates broken people who live in spiritually dark places. But those who live in the sunlight of God's presence are in vibrant, healthy places where they can grow and flourish.

Where do I go to get God's sunlight? You can get God's sunlight in the house of God, with God's people, and personally in the privacy of your own home. When we experience the presence of God and expose ourselves to His heavenly rays—as we worship Him—He inhabits and lives in our praise.

"But you are holy, you who inhabit the praises of Israel" (Psalm 22:3, NIV).

There have been many times in my life that I've been discouraged and depressed, but on Sunday morning, I get out of bed, put on some makeup and drive my car to God's house. I've entered those church doors emotionally and spiritually drained on numerous occasions, but once the worship team begins to praise God and I lift my voice and worship him–suddenly His Holy Spirit overshadows me, and the sunlight of his presence supernaturally fills me with His joy.

"You make known to me the path of life; in your presence is fullness of joy; at your right hand are pleasures forevermore" (Psalm 16:11, NLT).

I encourage you to be a part of an enthusiastic church with a lot of sunlight where you can experience the presence of God. When His sunlight comes into your life, darkness, sadness, and depression flee. Take time in your day to praise Him with your whole heart, listen to worship music—spend time soaking in His heavenly rays. You can experience Him by just being still and thinking of Him or thanking Him. You were created to enjoy the benefits of His glorious presence. He will fill your day with His joy as you spend time in His heavenly sunlight!

"For God, who said, let there be light in the darkness, has made this light shine in our hearts so we could know the glory of

God that is seen in the face of Jesus Christ" (2 Corinthians 4:6, NLT).

WATCH OVER YOUR VALUABLES

"Listen to another parable: There was a landowner who planted a vineyard. He put a wall around it, dug a winepress in it and built a watchtower" (Matthew 21:33, NIV).

There are many reasons to love California, but one of the valuable benefits of living here are the hundreds of vineyards that cover our landscape. Santa Rosa, Sonoma, and Napa Valley are known as the wine country and thousands of people travel from all over the world to come and enjoy it. This year I've driven through many cities that have acres and acres of these wonderful clusters of grapes. There are twenty wineries listed in the city of Morgan Hill where I live and a total of 4,653 in California. According to the 2016 Wine Institute, wine sales in the U.S. hit new records of $34.1 billion.

Imagine for a moment that you're an owner of one of these flourishing vineyards that dot the fertile soil in California and you're hoping to turn your grapes into a large crop. The money that you make from the harvest will provide for the needs of your family. Because you're a good farmer, you don't take your eyes off your field. You constantly watch over your plants and make sure they have all the best nutrients and tend to their growth and health. You watch for insects, birds and little foxes that attempt to steal your precious fruit.

God is speaking to you in this chapter about your future harvest and wants to show you how to be successful during the Summer season. He wants to teach you how to care for your investment and watch over your valuables. A good farmer doesn't take his eye off his fields. He monitors them and constantly evaluates his progress as it is growing.

Watch and Pray

"Watch and pray so that you will not give in to temptation. For the spirit is willing, but the body is weak" (Matthew 26:41, NLT).

Jesus taught us to watch and pray over our valuables. Are you praying daily for your life, family, ministry, business and spiritual life? Are you watching over the little foxes of bad habits, negative speech and ungodly relationships that influence your progress? Consider regular times for prayer, fasting, and pressing into God. Also get wise advice and counsel from godly people who love and care about you. Prayer and sound advice are essential as we watch over what is valuable in the Summer.

He Is Watching Over You

By the way, the Lord values you and is watching over you right now. Like a mother with her first baby—His loving eye is constantly on you. His eye is on the sparrow and you are far more valuable than a bird.

"Do not fear therefore; you are of more value than many sparrows" (Matthew 10:31, NKJV).

"He will cover you with His feathers, and under His wings you shall take refuge" (Psalm 91:4a, NIV).

Whatever She Does Shall Prosper

Every Summer our church has a two-week program for teenagers who make a one-year commitment to serve as interns in our Youth Ministry. I've had the privilege of speaking and sharing stories about my life as a Pastor's wife with them. They're usually more interested in asking questions about my personal life than they are about the deep spiritual lessons I want to teach them.

My son, Jordan, loves being their youth pastor and spends many hours investing in their young lives. At the end of our sessions, they can ask any questions about the Bible, their life or any topic of their choosing. They always want me to tell them stories about the worst things Jordan did during his childhood. It gives me great pleasure to relive and tell them Jordan's dastardly deeds as a child. Smile.

I love to talk to them about the wonderful plans God has for their future and how they can have a blessed life. It's also great to take them to the book of Psalms and show them how much God wants to prosper them. I let them know they will have to work hard to catch the little foxes that keep them from accomplishing God's purpose for their lives.

"Blessed is the one who does not walk in step with the wicked or stand in the way that sinners take or sit in the company of mockers, but whose delight is in the law of the Lord and meditates on his law day and night. That person will be like a tree planted by the streams of water, which yields fruit in its season, whose leaf does not wither; and whatever they do will prosper" (Psalm 1:1-3, NIV).

In one session, I asked them if they've seen the commercial, "You can learn a lot from a dummy." The dummies get behind the wheel of a car and simulate a crash test without wearing a seat belt and the dummy flies through the windshield. I said: "Did you know you can learn a lot from a dummy? You really can learn a lot from watching stupid people who eventually destroy their lives because of wrong choices they make. Or you can learn by watching wise people who build their lives on the firm foundation of God's Word."

I asked the twenty teenagers another a question—"How many of you want the blessings of God on your life?" All of them raised their hands in agreement and wanted to know how to acquire His blessings.

I continued to share with them: "Just because you are surrounded with ungodly people at home, at work, or school doesn't mean you have to follow what they are doing; you can choose to go in a different direction and listen to godly people who will give you wisdom. Jesus intentionally appointed you for greatness. The people you choose now for friends will determine your future. Show me who your friends are, and I will tell you your future." 2 Timothy says pursue righteous people who call on His name.

"Flee also youthful lusts; but pursue righteousness, faith, love, peace with those who call on the Lord out of a pure heart" (2 Timothy 2:22, NKJV).

Women who pursue righteousness and learn from those who have a pure heart are on their way to a fruitful harvest. Psalm 1 says we can be blessed if we listen to wise counsel and delight in His Word. But to bring forth fruit in due season, we must catch the little foxes of unbelief and listen to the godly voices who guide our lives.

"Our vineyards are in blossom: we must catch the little foxes that destroy the vineyards" (Song of Solomon 2:15, CEV).

Jesus said there are two kinds of women: the wise woman and the foolish woman. A wise woman who builds her house on the foundation of His Word is likened to a wise builder. She is still standing, after the floods and the winds beat on her house because she listens to His voice. She can weather the harsh storms of the Summer because her foundation is built on the Word of God.

"Therefore, whoever hears these sayings of Mine, and does them, I will liken him to a wise man who built his house on the rock; and the rain descended, the floods came, and the winds blew and beat on that house; and it did not fall, for it was founded on the rock. But everyone who hears these sayings of Mine, and does not do them, will be like a foolish man who built his house on the sand. And the rain descended, the floods came, and the winds blew and beat on that house, and it fell. And great was the fall" (Matthew 7:24-27, NKJV).

We Weather Hardships

Summer can be a taxing time, especially if we are working through difficult times. Harvest never comes apart from hardship. Summer storms can be violent and Summer heat unbearable. Difficult times come to our lives—financial setbacks, accidents, illness, and death. Still, great women weather hardships and experience a harvest because they don't give up in the hard times.

"And let us not grow weary while doing good, for in due season we shall reap if we do not lose heart" (Galatians 6:9, NKJV).

We Weather Failures

Facing failure well is one of the most important lessons we can learn during the Summer season. Everyone fails at one time or another, even good women—the key is to learn from our mistakes and not to repeat them—then we can move forward. God loves failures—Jesus died for goof-ups and fools. Aren't you glad He picks us up every time we fall?

"For a righteous man may fall seven times and rise again, but the wicked shall fall by calamity" (Proverbs 24:16, NKJV).

One of the things I have struggled with is my tendency to speak before I think. Can you relate? Have you ever said something and instantly regretted it even as it was coming out of your mouth? This happens to me on a regular basis. I get irritated and impatient with people and say unkind words. I fail, but I can rise again. I know if I confess my faults to Him, He will faithfully forgive and cleanse me from all unrighteousness.

"If we confess our sins, He is faithful and just to forgive us our sins and to cleanse us from all unrighteousness" (I John 1:9, KJV).

We Weather Discouragement

I was so excited when I learned that I was pregnant with my first son in the early years of my marriage. I was very aware that I didn't know the first thing about being a good mom and began to rehearse all the things I didn't know how to do. Back in my twenties, I had a bad habit of saying "I can't do it." If a situation seemed too hard, my initial response was, "I can't do it." When I brought my newborn baby home from the hospital and had to wake up to him crying in the middle of the night to change his diaper and feed him—that was hard work. I wasn't in the habit of waking up two and three times a night. I didn't think I was going to make it through the first week of motherhood.

I cried to my husband, "I can't do it." I got so discouraged with the sleepless nights and learning how to care for a newborn. After a few years of living with me, he said, "Do you know how many times a day you say, "I can't do it?" I didn't realize that my words were feeding my discouragement and hindering me from believing God's Word.

Philippians 4:13 says "I can do all things through Christ who strengthens me." I was trying to live my life in my own strength—that was my problem. I am now teaching myself to say, "I can do ALL things through Christ who strengthens me."

When we make Jesus the center of every part of our lives, including getting up in the middle of the night with hungry babies, He will strengthen us. We can do all things through Christ. I had to remember that He is the Vine and I am the branch—when I live in Him, I will be very productive.

We Weather Impatience

In this day of fast-paced living, high-speed Internet, fast food, and fast cars—we want everything as soon as possible. Online shopping has made things incredibly convenient and with a touch of a button, we can request a package to be delivered to our home the next day. Unfortunately, the Kingdom of God doesn't work that way. God doesn't move in our lives as fast as our high-speed Internet service. His plans and purposes for our lives are long-term, and He has a much bigger plan than we can imagine. Be patient, fruit takes time to grow and you can't hurry the harvest, but it will come if you just hang in there. Don't be so hard on yourself—He is working in your heart—there is no such thing as instant success, but as you continue to sow, you will reap.

"Wait patiently for the master's arrival. You see farmers do this all the time, waiting for their valuable crops to mature, patiently letting the rain do its slow but sure work. Be patient like that. Stay steady and strong" (James 5:7-8, MSG).

Here's the principle in the Kingdom of God: "Water, plant, grow!" Remember—Jesus chose and appointed you to produce long-lasting fruit.

"You did not choose me, but I chose you and appointed you that you should go and bear fruit, and that your fruit should remain, that whatever you ask the Father in My name He may give you" (John 15:16, NKJV).

You've come through your Winter season, you've planted your Spring seed, the sun is beating down during your Summer, giving the nourishment your soul needs. You are nearing your harvest. It might be hot and sticky, but don't take a vacation from God now! Now is your time of working, watering, watching and weathering. Your harvest is close so let your perspiration and hard work prepare you for celebration!

Discussion Questions

Open Up: How do you stay connected to Jesus in your daily life?

Share Scriptures: Let different members/friends share a verse or idea from this chapter that impacted them personally. What does it mean for you?

Talk It Over: How do women grow in their Summer season? Why do you think it's important to be planted in a great church?

Pray Together: Pray for each other to not give up during difficult seasons.

Prayer for the Summer Season:

Father God, you have been so faithful to me through my Summer season. I will not give up and I will not grow weary! I am ready to enter a new season of harvest. I ask you for strength and the power of the Holy Spirit to overcome my failures, discouragement, and impatience. Accelerate your Kingdom purpose in me. In Christ's Name, AMEN.

5
THE COLORS ARE ABOUT TO CHANGE

He changes times and seasons; he deposes kings and raises up others. He gives wisdom to the wise and knowledge to the discerning.

Daniel 2:21(NIV)

It is easy to see with our natural eye when one season is ending and another one is quickly approaching. The Summer season has just ended in California and the weather is finally cooling down, the air is crisp, and the leaves are changing their colors. I look forward to the Fall season because I can start making plans for the Thanksgiving holiday and that means quality time with my family. I can count on the season changing in the first part of November like clockwork and know it is time to start unpacking my sweaters and boots and putting away my Summer clothes.

In the first book of the Bible God made a promise to Noah and his family after they survived the flood. He said that they would always be able to depend on the consistent seasonal changes.

"While the earth remains, seedtime and harvest, cold and heat, winter and summer, and day and night shall not cease" (Genesis 8:22, NKJV).

In other words, He is saying: "The seasons will always change but you can trust Me to keep the earth running in an orderly fashion." God also wants us to understand that seasons change according to His unfolding plan and purpose for us.

"For everything there is a season, a time for every purpose under heaven: a time to be born, a time to die; a time to plant, a time to pluck that which is planted; a time to kill, a time to heal; a time to break down, a time to build up, a time to weep, a time to laugh, a time to mourn, a time to dance; a time to cast away stones, and a time to gather stones; a time to embrace, a time to refrain from embracing, a time to seek, and a time to lose, a time to keep, a time to cast away, a time to rend, a time to sew, a time to keep silence, a time to speak; a time to love, a time to hate; a time for war, and a time for peace" (Ecclesiastes 3:2-8, ASV).

As I mentioned in Chapter One, *Understanding Natural and Spiritual Seasons*, I'm a person who likes the security and stability of knowing when one season is ending, and another is about to begin. I like planning ahead for the predictable changes, but it's a different story when unexpected circumstances happen and I'm unsure of my future.

I've heard some women say, "Why doesn't God just give me a blueprint and tell me exactly what He has planned for my life?" God, in His infinite wisdom, chooses to teach us through the beauty of various seasons rather than give us His entire plan all at once. Our relationship with Him is based on our complete trust in His Word and our faith in Him—in what His specific plans are for us.

Have you ever had a time in your life when someone overwhelmed you with troubling news? Maybe it came from your doctor, your husband, or your employer. Did the news create feelings of turmoil and fear in your heart? Did it make you question whether God understood what was happening to you? I don't really appreciate someone (my husband)—or God—turning my stable world upside down, especially when it means leaving the comfort of my neatly laid plans. If you've been through these disturbing moments, then this chapter is for you.

In January of 1986, my husband and I scraped every nickel together to save for airline tickets to the Philippine Islands. Our church was sending him to create a promotional video for our

Missions Department. My sister, Lisa, and her husband, Bill, were sent there by our church to serve as missionaries and I really wanted to go along and visit her. It was so wonderful to see what the founders of Philippine Miracle Mission had built in thirty years. The Children's home, the Bible college, and the churches were all growing, and we would have the privilege of supporting them with their vision.

Our trip to the Philippines was a successful one and we arrived home safely to our happy life in California. My husband began working on the fundraising video and dove back into his work at the church. I was so excited to be back home with my little son, Aaron, and I was feeling the normal symptoms of being three months pregnant with my second son, Jordan.

I was enjoying our new home that my husband worked so diligently to remodel and make comfortable for our growing family. I had such a great time decorating the baby's nursery with a cute comforter and primary colored cars. I wanted to make sure everything was perfect for his arrival to our family.

I loved my new neighborhood and memorized the routes to the grocery store, the coffee shop and, of course, my hairdresser. I knew how long it would take me to drive down Meridian Avenue to get to church. I was feeling settled in my new home and everything was perfect until my husband told me the exciting revelation he received from God one day in his early morning prayers. He said: "I've been praying, and I feel God is calling us to be missionaries to the Philippines." My settled, perfect world just came to a screeching halt with those few words. Just like that, everything that we had worked so hard to accomplish was being interrupted by an unforeseen force.

Now, I'm not proud of my initial response to this call to a foreign land. You must understand my thoughts, moving my family to the Philippines was not my idea, nor was it a part of the dream I had for my future. I responded to my husband with great intensity, "You realize that we just remodeled our home and it's the way we like it. We have a two-year-old and I'm four months pregnant? This is not a good time for you to spring this kind of news on me. Seriously, you heard God say He is calling us to the Philippines? He may have told you that you are called, but He didn't say anything to me!"

When I'm told that my season is about to change, especially when it's not my idea, I need some time to process and agree with this change. My prayers were filled with questions and I asked God: "Why would you ask someone like me to be a missionary? I don't know the first thing about being a missionary." I was just getting comfortable with being a new wife and mother. I didn't want to make a life-changing move to a foreign country.

Looking back over the seasons of our married life, being part of what he [my husband] feels God is calling Him to do has truly been an adventure. Most of these adventures have not been my ideas—adventures that don't include my comfort or stability—and haven't usually gone over too well in the initial conversations.

I'm not going to lie and say angels were singing and I heard a voice from heaven about moving to the Philippines. I didn't have the same experience as Mary, the mother of Jesus, who was told by an angel, "Mary, rejoice, highly favored one, the Lord is with you; blessed are you among women!" (Luke 1:28) I did eventually get comfortable with the idea that God could use me to be a missionary and I began to believe God was speaking to me, too. I did experience a deep peace in my heart.

There are other women in the Bible such as Sarah, the mother of our faith, who didn't react perfectly to their husband's revelations from God, either. I'm sure when Abraham told Sarah, "I don't know where we're going honey, but I know it's to a land whose maker and builder is God." Huh? (Hebrews 11:10) I wonder if Sarah was envisioning something different for her life when she married Abraham. Or when he said: "Sweetheart, it will be all right, just tell them you're my sister, so I will be treated well for your sake and my life will be spared because of you." (Genesis 12:13) I can only imagine that she may have had some questions for God when she was moving in with Pharaoh.

When God called Sarah to conceive a child as a ninety-something woman, she laughed out loud. (Genesis 18:10-15) Of course, she had a few spicy moments and mistakes of her own, but we won't go into those here. We're talking about visionary men, like my husband and Abraham, and how it affects their women, remember?

Have you ever felt like Mary and questioned God? Or laughed like Sarah and wondered why God was calling you to do something totally crazy for Him far beyond your natural abilities? I'm so glad God shared the stories of real women in the Bible who struggled with God's call on their lives. Their real-life stories encourage us to follow their example of faith and how they trusted God to fulfill the promises He made to them. Mary's acceptance of God's favor on her life made her the mother of the Savior of the world. (Luke 1:38) Sarah's belief in God made her the mother of a great and mighty nation. (Genesis 18:18; Hebrews 11:11)

God uses changing seasons to show us He has a purpose for every event in our lives. He will challenge us to do things we never thought we could do. He will take us to places that we couldn't possibly go in our own strength. He wants to show up big-time in our lives when our season abruptly changes and it's totally out of our control.

There is a theme throughout the Bible: God calls ordinary women to do extraordinary things for Him. Most of them had questions and considered it unthinkable that they could ever fulfill their calling. They didn't understand why God would want to use them because they were trusting in their own limited abilities. God wanted to broaden their vision and help them to see their unlimited potential in Him. You may have voiced some of your own reasons why God would not want to call you:

- I'm not qualified
- I'm not educated
- I'm not from the right family
- I've made too many mistakes
- I have too many emotional issues - fear, anger, depression
- I'm too young - I'm too old
- I'm divorced - I'm single

I'm proof that God can use anyone He chooses and can do amazing things through ordinary women who are willing to put their complete trust in Him. As women of God, we must stop looking at our limitations and believe that God is leading by the Holy Spirit to empower and strengthen us to move into our new season. Moving forward, however, will require us to get rid of some old, negative thinking and replace it with new thinking.

OUT WITH THE OLD — IN WITH THE NEW

It's amazing how many old knick-knacks, out-of-style clothes, letters from old lovers, and outdated jewelry women collect. Nobody likes the long, difficult process of moving from one place to another. It means collecting boxes, old newspapers, bubble wrap, and tape, then we painstakingly wrap each item to be packed. If there's somebody out there who enjoys this process, please call me and volunteer at my next moving party.

Have you ever packed up outdated clothing and ugly plates that you haven't used in the last ten years? Then moved those belongings to another house, only to find out you didn't use them in the next ten years? And why? Because there's a small chance you might need them?

We sometimes create the same scenario in our spiritual and emotional lives when we pack up old, hurtful memories and drag them with us. We do it because we think they will bring us stability. After all, it's been our "normal," and although destructive, there's comfort in knowing what's there, what's a constant. We let them consume our thought lives and focusing on the hurtful past rather than spending time in God's Word to "know the truth" and be set free.

I encourage you to get rid of the old things you're not going to use in your new season. Ask God what needs to be left behind. Ask Him what lies ahead and begin each day with excited anticipation. He will provide His treasures to fill up the new spaces.

How do we embrace the new and get rid of the old? We must stop focusing on all the things that hinder us from moving forward and start setting our sights on the heavenly life Christ wants us to experience.

"Since you have been raised to new life with Christ, set your sights on the realities of heaven, where Christ sits in the place of honor at God's right hand. Think about the things of heaven, not the things of earth. For you died to this life, and your real life is hidden with Christ in God. And when Christ, who is your life, is revealed to the whole world, you will share in all his glory" (Colossians 3: 1-3, NLT).

Consider Mary, the mother of Jesus, and the extraordinary season change in her young life. She had a supernatural visit by the angel Gabriel who brought her some startling news. Imagine her hearing that God called her to become pregnant by the Holy Spirit. She had never been sexually intimate with a man, so she wondered how this could be possible. (Matthew 1:23; 2:15; and 3:17)

The backdrop of this story is set in a time when young peasant girls weren't trained to study the Scriptures, but they were brought up to be housewives. Mary asked a reasonable question that any intelligent woman in her predicament would be asking—how can this be since I've never slept with a man?

"In the six-month of Elizabeth's pregnancy, God sent the angel Gabriel to the Galilean Village of Nazareth to a virgin engaged to be married to a man descended from David. His name was Joseph, and the virgin's name, Mary. Gabriel greeted her:

Good morning! You are beautiful with God's beauty! Beautiful inside and out! God be with you. She was thoroughly shaken, wondering what was behind a greeting like that. But the angel assured her, 'Mary, you have nothing to fear. God has a surprise for you: you will become pregnant and give birth to a son and call his name Jesus. He will be great, be called *Son of the Highest.* The Lord God will give him the throne of his father David; he will rule Jacob's house forever—no end, ever, to his kingdom.' Mary said to the angel, 'But how? I've never slept with a man'" (Luke 1:26-34, MSG).

If you are sensing change is coming because you were approached by an angel, your husband, or your boss, then you might be troubled and ask natural questions like Mary: "How can this be when I'm not equipped to carry out this task?" God has the answers to your questions and you can find some of them by reading the amazing story of Mary, the mother of Jesus. God called Mary to do the impossible because He knew how she would respond to His calling. A big part of Mary's success was due to her agreement with God's plan for her life; her response was to trust and obey.

The first answer to Mary's sincere question comes when the angel Gabriel greets Mary. He says she is highly favored and blessed because the Lord is with her. Then he repeats it again and says, "Don't be afraid because you have found favor with God."

God is looking for women young and old who will believe what He says about them: that they are highly favored and blessed because they are His. What does it mean to be highly favored and blessed? To be highly favored is to be graced to obey God's will. It means that He accepts and appoints you to do great things for Him because you choose to obey Him.

"To the praise and the glory of His name by which He made us accepted in the Beloved" (Ephesians 1:6, NKJV).

Being favored by God enables us by the Holy Spirit to exhibit qualities we wouldn't ordinarily have: sweetness, charm, loveliness, joy, delight, a thankful disposition. Do you believe that God called a young girl to raise Jesus in her family, so He could one day love us and forgive us of our sins? Do you believe that God is with you and you are highly favored? God wants you to stop looking at your impossibilities and believe that the Holy Spirit will come and overshadow you with His power.

The angel Gabriel also encouraged Mary, not only is she highly favored, but the power of the Holy Spirit will overshadow her and enable her to do the impossible, for nothing is impossible with God.

"And the angel answered and said to her, "The Holy Spirit will come upon you and the power of the Highest will overshadow you... for with God nothing will be impossible." Then Mary said, "Behold the maidservant of the Lord! Let it be to me according to your Word." And the angel departed from her" (Luke 1:35-38, NKJV).

God is guiding every changing season in your life and has chosen you for a specific purpose in His perfect timing. He will guide you, empower you, and enable you with His favor when you believe that nothing is impossible with Him.

Do you need God's power to overshadow you today for an impossible task or situation? Come into agreement with the promises He's made you and respond like Mary did: "Let it be to me according to your will."

HE WILL GUIDE YOU WITH PERFECT PEACE

"For the Kingdom of God is not eating and drinking, but righteousness and peace and joy in the Holy Spirit" (Romans 14:17, NKJV).

I needed God's power to overshadow me as I wrestled with the idea of going to the Philippines. As a young mother of two small children, I knew I had to get direction and strength from God. I had to know, beyond a shadow of a doubt, that He wanted me to move my newborn baby and my three-year-old to a foreign country. Trust me, I could not have moved to the other side of the world without God doing a miracle in my heart.

After I finished ranting and raving about the many reasons God couldn't possibly be calling me, I shifted my focus from me to Him and began searching the Scriptures for answers. I prayed and asked God to guide me by His Word instead of my wavering emotions.

"For this reason, I am telling you, whatever you ask for in prayer, believe (trust and be confident) that it is granted to you, and you will [get it]" (Mark 11:24, AMP).

I began to pray, telling Him I would be willing to go if He would take the nauseous feeling out of the pit of my stomach. I said: "God, okay, I give this desire that my husband has to you. If you want me to go, you have to change my heart and give me your peace." I would then know that He wanted me to go on this adventure if I had His peace—and I mean total peace. And you know what? I felt God's supernatural peace and I started to feel excited about going on this adventure. He filled my heart with His love for the Filipino people. My husband and I thought we were going there to see God do great things... and we did.

We sold our newly decorated home and I left the comfort zone of my quaint little neighborhood and familiar places. Packing up my earthly belongings, I did not know if I would return to California. My husband and I had to choose very carefully the few items that were totally necessary to take with us to our new home. We didn't have room for anything that wasn't going to be beneficial to us on our journey of faith. At this point, I didn't have the luxury of bringing my old fear-filled thinking. If I was going to move forward I had to believe I was highly favored and the Holy Spirit would overshadow me.

I learned that God had a purpose for our changing season. It wasn't just about living in the Philippines, but it was also about the great things God did in our hearts. He showed us how He was guiding with His peace, prospering us and making us fruitful in this wonderful season of change in our lives.

One of the ways God will lead you is when you allow His peace to rule in your heart. He will give you a sense of His joy when He wants you to step out in faith and accomplish amazing things for Him.

"And let the peace that comes from Christ rule in your hearts. For as members of one body you are called to live in peace. And always be thankful" (Colossians 3:15, NLT).

If you see the colors changing in your season, remember God's love never changes and He promises to keep you in perfect peace as you enter your Fall season. Meditate on the following Scripture and let God's peace wash over you as you put your trust in Him. God may not be calling you to be a missionary to a foreign country, but He is calling you to believe the promises He's made to you in His Word for your next season.

"He will keep in perfect peace all those who trust in Him, whose thoughts turn often to the Lord" (Isaiah 26:3, TLB)!

Discussion Questions

Open Up: Share a time when you were surprised by a season of change.

Share Scriptures: Let different members/friends share a verse or idea from this chapter that impacted them personally. What does it mean for you?

Talk It Over: How does God lead us through seasons of change?

Pray Together: Pray for each other to believe God's promises in every season.

    Prayer for the Changing Season:

Father God, you have seated me in heavenly places with you. Help me to remember to think about things that are in heaven. Thank you for guiding me with your peace through my season of change. In Christ's Name, AMEN.

6
A TIME FOR FULFILLMENT

To everything there is a season…
a time to laugh… a time to dance
Ecclesiastes 3:1, 4 (KJV)

For some, the Fall season is a time when people love to travel to the East Coast to places like New England, Maine, and Massachusetts to view the vibrant foliage that is transforming into beautiful colors of gold, red, purple, burgundy and orange.

Did I mention that Fall is one of my favorite seasons of the year because it's time for pumpkin, spice lattes and, of course, sweet potato pie, butternut squash soup, and apple cinnamon cobbler to celebrate the harvest season? All these festivities are wonderful moments to enjoy with family and friends, but there's something more God wants us to experience.

A woman who is in her Fall Season may be seeing answers to her prayers and her loved ones coming to know the Lord. Autumn is when she's finally reaping what she's sown and is enjoying the fruit in her own character, better relationships with her family, and more success in her financial ventures.

In the previous chapters of this book, you met some strong, courageous women, like Cari and Naomi, who survived the subzero temperatures of their Winter season and chose to be inspired to dream again. Karen and Helen took advantage of the new opportunities in their Spring season and prepared themselves for their future harvest. Joanne and Carol weathered the warm Summer heat and began to see increase and growth in their relationships with God.

In this chapter, you'll be introduced to some brave women who had unexpected surprises entering their Fall season, but they made the right choices that brought them into a time of joy and fulfillment. All their sowing, watering, working and waiting through every cycle finally brought them a harvest of joy.

I want you to imagine you're a young widow of a farming family and you've survived a tough year. Your children look tired and hungry, but in your hand is the bag of grain that can feed your family. You reassure your hungry children they're going to be just fine, but instead of crushing the grain to make bread, you plant those seeds in the soil.

You're weeping while you plant those seeds, wondering what you're going to do until those seeds become a harvest in the Fall. You know from experience, if you're going to feed your children next Winter, you'll have to part with your precious seed today. You see the harvest in your mind's eye--tall, ripened, and abundant. You wipe your face and sow your seed, knowing you'll receive a bountiful crop from the few seeds you have sown. Your silent tears will finally become joyous and jubilant laughter.

The book of Psalms records a promise of joy to women who sow in tears:

"Those who sow in tears will reap with shouts of joy. The one that goes along weeping, carrying the bag of seed, she will surely come back with shouts of joy, carrying her sheaves" (Psalm 126:5-6, ESV).

IT'S TIME TO CELEBRATE

Fall is a time for celebration and fulfillment because God has faithfully rewarded your trust in Him. He has promised you time and again in His Word, whatever is perpetually sown, will ultimately be reaped. When you plant those tiny little seeds of faith underground, where they're not visible, you must trust that God is going to continue His work in your life.

The following Scripture tells us that a woman who continually plants good seed will be rewarded for not giving up and will reap good things in her life at the right time.

"Do not be misled: no one makes a fool of God. What a person plants, she will harvest. The person who plants selfishness, ignoring the needs of others—ignoring God—harvests a crop of weeds. All she'll have to show for her life is weeds! But the one who plants in response to God, letting God's Spirit do the growth work in her, will harvest a crop of real life, eternal life. So, let's not allow ourselves to get fatigued doing good. At the right time, we will harvest a good crop if we don't give up or quit" (Galatians 6:7-9, MSG).

I want to encourage you today: God is going to bring good things into your life that will bring you satisfaction. Every good seed that you've planted will take root and grow, but it will take His timing for you to see a bountiful harvest come back to you: saved souls in your family, a change in your character, better relationships, or more financial blessings in your business. No farmer plants one day and expects a full grove of cherry trees or a field of lettuce the next day. In the same way, it takes time for the spiritual seeds of love, patience, and forgiveness to be multiplied and come back to you in a miraculous crop of blessings. God is a promise-keeping, covenant-honoring God; you can't control the season you're in, but you can choose to believe that God will fulfill His promises.

Don't quit, but think about the faithful, godly women who kept believing the promises of God even when times were rough. They came into their harvest season and are enjoying the results of their diligent work.

There's a principle in the Bible—when you've spent decades tending your garden and you see a tremendous amount fruit, you shouldn't be surprised. If you've raised your kids in the ways of God and they become successful, happy people; that did not happen by accident. There is a reason my sons love the Lord with all their heart. I believe it's due to the many years of diligent work that my husband and I have put into them. We consistently made a point of sowing good seeds into their hearts. Were we the perfect parents? Absolutely not, but we were serious about living our lives for God in our home and we're reaping the benefits of putting His Word into practice.

There are rewards for being a good and faithful steward of the things God has entrusted to you. Jesus commended the trustworthy servants in Matthew 25:23 for being loyal over the small responsibilities He gave to them and He rewarded them for their faithfulness. He told them because you've been faithful over a few things, I will put you in charge of many things. He invited them to enter the joy of the Lord. I love the way the New International Version says it:

"His master replied, 'Well done good and faithful servant! You have been faithful with a few things; I will put you in charge of many things. Come and share your master's happiness' (Matthew 25:21, NIV)!

Lift Up Your Eyes

Fall is a wonderful time of year because God opens your eyes to see what He sees. There's always an opportunity for a harvest season and often it's right in front of you. Jesus told his disciples to look up and see the ripened fields that were ready for harvest.

"Do you not say, there are still four months and then comes the harvest? Behold, I say to you, lift up your eyes and look at the fields, for they are already white for harvest" (John 4:35-36, NKJV).

Let's look back at the *Spring Season*, in Chapter Three. We read the familiar story in the Book of John when Jesus taught His disciples to "lift up" their eyes and see their future harvest. Remember when He was talking with a Samaritan woman at Jacob's well? He illustrated what can happen when we get our eyes off our natural circumstances and open them to the opportunities God has right in front of us.

"Just then his disciples returned and were surprised to find him talking with a woman. But no one asked, 'What do you want?' or, 'Why are you talking with her?' Then, leaving her water jar, the woman went back to the town and said to the people, come, see a man who told me everything I ever did. Could this be the Messiah? They came out of the town and made their way toward him. Meanwhile, the disciples urged him, Rabbi, eat something. But he said to them, I have food to eat that you know nothing about. Then the disciples said to each other, could someone have brought him food? My food, said Jesus, is to do the will of Him who sent me and finish His work" (John 4:27-34, NIV).

You may recall how surprised the disciples were that Jesus was talking to this Samaritan woman, and how they asked why He was talking to her. Everything that Jesus does has a purpose and He wants to broaden our mindset: He crossed cultural and religious barriers—talking to a Samaritan woman just wasn't done in those days.

It's interesting to note that the disciples were focused on the fact that Jesus didn't eat lunch and were wondering if anyone had brought Him anything to eat. But Jesus redirected them and explained why he was talking to this woman. He told them He wasn't worried about eating lunch and filling His belly with food, but He was getting His fulfillment from doing His Father's work.

It's Harvest Time

Jesus was about to give them a live illustration of why He was talking to the Samaritan woman. He didn't walk to Jacob's well that day just because he was thirsty, and he didn't come down from heaven just to be a carpenter. He was saying: Guys, watch and learn from what I'm about to teach you next. I'm going to show you My Father's work in living color.

"Do you not say, there are still four months and then comes the harvest? Behold, I say to you, open your eyes and look at the fields, for they are already white for harvest! And he who reaps receives wages and gathers fruit for eternal life, that both he who sows and he who reaps may rejoice together. For in this saying it is true: one sows, and another reaps. I sent you to reap that for which you have not labored; others have labored, and you have entered into their labors" (John 4:35-38, NKJV).

Loving people is at the top of Jesus' priority list—He was reaping the Samaritan woman, so to speak, right before the disciples' eyes. She was a part of the white fields that were ready to be picked.

This lonely woman's trip to the well that day made a way for many in the city of Samaria to be introduced to the light of the world and believe that Jesus was their Savior. Jesus wants us to see beyond our day-to-day-lives and open our eyes to our friends, co-workers and loved ones that are ready to come into the Kingdom of God.

I wonder if we're seeing what Jesus wants us to see today—the harvests in our "now," especially people who are open to the Lord. Or could we be like the disciples, too focused on "someday" and "tomorrow?" Today is the day of harvest if we'll open our eyes to see what Jesus sees.

"And many of the Samaritans of that city believed in Him because of the word of the woman who testified, He told me all that I ever did. So, when the Samaritans had come to Him and they urged Him to stay with them; and He stayed there two days. And many more believed because of His own Word. Then they said to the woman, now we believe, not because of what you said, for we ourselves have heard Him and we know that this is indeed the Christ, the savior of the world" (John 4:39-42, NKJV).

The day Jesus walked to Jacob's well was the day He brought His light into a place where people were living in darkness. Perhaps you're aware that we're living in a time of great darkness and there are hurting people all around us desperately in need of God's love. Jesus said that angels rejoice every time a person who's living in darkness turns their life around and follows Him. He was so happy when the Samaritan woman and many of her friends realized why Jesus came into their city that day.

"In the same way, I tell you, there is rejoicing in the presence of angels of God over one sinner who repents" (Luke 15:10, NIV).

It's Time to Rejoice

"The people who walked in darkness have seen a great light... You [oh Lord] have multiplied the nation and increased their joy; they rejoice before You, like the joy in harvest" (Isaiah 9:2-3, AMP).

This passage predicts the ministry of Jesus and the light He brought to Israel, but it includes a lesson beyond that: Faith moves beyond the darkness with shouts of harvest joy!

I'm not a farmer, but I can imagine what it must feel like to work all season long, planting seeds, hoping for a plentiful harvest. It must be exciting for a farmer to see acres and acres of fruitful trees ready to be picked. In the same way, when you see your prayers answered and your precious crops are finally brought in, it's a time to jump for joy. There's a sense of satisfaction and accomplishment that needs to find expression in your life when you realize your goals. When God's promise becomes reality, you too will enter the joy of harvest and a supernatural celebration will take place!

I've learned a lot of important lessons from watching the brave single moms who have been a part of my life. I recently heard a story of a woman who was in a very dark place in her life. She didn't know how she was going to survive one more day without any money to take care of her son or pay her rent. How was she going to feed her starving son when she was down to her last dollar? Her sad story made me think of the unnamed widow in the Bible, who also went through a long season of lack, but something miraculous happened to move her into a season of blessing.

In this new age of social media, I've been tempted to idolize the wealthy, beautiful women who are praised in the world's spotlight. If you're like me, you want to know how they arrived at the place of success and what steps they followed to get to their season of harvest. But God has a much better way to make us prosper. If we'll follow His ways, we'll grow and be unbelievably fruitful.

"My thoughts are nothing like your thoughts, says the Lord. And My ways are far beyond anything you could imagine. For just as the heavens are higher than the earth, so My ways are higher than your ways and my thoughts are higher than your thoughts. The rain and snow come down from the heavens and stay on the ground to water the earth. They cause the grain to grow, producing seed for the farmer and bread for the hungry. It is the same with my Word. I send it out, and it always produces fruit. It will accomplish all I want it to, and it will prosper everywhere I send it" (Isaiah 55:8-1, NLT).

FALL IS A TIME TO SHARE

Most women I know love to share and give to others, but what do we do about the dark times when we barely have enough to share with our own families? What did the widow of Zarephath do when she and her son were down to their last meal, ready to die? What could she do when the King of her country was leading them down a path to destruction?

"Then the Word of the Lord came to him, saying, Arise, go to Zarephath, which belongs to Sidon, and dwell there. See, I have commanded the widow there to provide for you. So, he arose and went to Zarephath. And when he came to the gate of the city, indeed a widow was there gathering sticks. And he called her and said, please bring me a little water in a cup that I may drink. And as she was going to get it, he called to her and said, please bring me a morsel of bread in your hand. So, she said, as the Lord your God lives, I do not have bread, only a handful of flour in a bin, and a little oil in a jar; and see, I am gathering a couple of sticks that I may go in and prepare it for myself and my son, that we may eat it, and die. And Elijah said to her, do not fear, go do as you have said, but make me a small cake first, and bring it to me; and afterward make some for yourself and your son. For thus says the Lord God of Israel: the bin of flour shall not be used up, nor shall the jar of the oil run dry, until the Lord sends rain on the earth. So, she went away and did according to the Word of Elijah; and she and her household ate for many days. The bin of flour was not used up, nor did the jar of oil run dry, according to the Word of the Lord which He spoke by Elijah" (1 Kings 16:8-16, NKJV).

I wonder how the widow woman felt as she used the last of her flour? I imagine she was like any other loving mother who wants the best for her children—to be able to provide everything they need. She was not only having a bad day, but the land had been in severe drought for years. Her life was about to be changed when a prophet named Elijah came walking through the gates of her city.

The widow was living in a day and age when women were totally dependent on the men in their lives to take care of them. The women in her village bought their food from the nearby farms and relied on the rain to water crops to feed their families. She had no food and very little water–there were no food shelters or government agencies she could go to for help. She didn't choose the season of surprise that happened to her, but God had plans to provide for all her needs.

The setting of her unbelievable story is placed in a village in the northern kingdom of Israel; the land was in a three and one-half year drought due to the actions of an idolatrous king. The Bible says that King Ahab did evil in the sight of the Lord, more than all the other kings who were before him. (1 Kings 16:30) He and his wife Jezebel set up an altar to worship the wooden image of Baal; those who worshipped Baal believed he controlled the rain.

God used the prophet Elijah during this time in history to predict that a drought would come over the land. Elijah prayed that the rain would stop to send a message that the God of Israel controlled the weather, not Baal. We're told in Ephesians 5:16-18 that Elijah was an ordinary human just like us, but when he earnestly prayed, the rain stopped for three and one-half years. His prophetic declaration of drought affected the entire region.

The drought in Israel didn't compare to the four-year drought California recently experienced. The water supply was looking grim and in short supply, but we still had food, bottled water, and government assistance. Anyone who was in desperate need could still go to a food bank for a hot meal and something to drink.

The widow wasn't expecting much from her limited circumstances and she couldn't see beyond her empty cupboards. She was preparing her last meal and getting ready to die when Elijah came walking into her village.

Elijah had the audacity to ask her for her last meal and something to drink. He could see that she was gathering sticks and she told him her plans to cook one more meal for her son. In other words, she was saying: isn't it obvious, I don't have enough to share with you? I only have a little bit and then we're going to die—that's my plan and I can see no way out of this mess. Elijah told her not to be afraid—He knew something she didn't know—and He was following God's lead on this one.

We can see throughout the Bible that God takes care of women who are in great darkness. He highlights them as heroes of faith that we can draw our inspiration from in our times of need.

I believe that He wants to bless you and make you abundantly fruitful like the widow woman. Deuteronomy 15:10 tells us how you can make sure you'll have more than enough for your family and have leftovers to share. Just look at what the Bible says will happen to you as you generously give to Him.

"Give generously to Him and do so without a grudging heart; then because of this, the Lord your God will bless you and all your work and in everything you put your hand" (Deuteronomy 15:10, NIV).

Can you relate to the widow woman? Are you looking at what you don't have in your cupboards? Are you ready to give up? Bring Him your cup of water and your little bit of flour—act on God's promises to you—your flour bin won't go empty and your jar of oil won't run dry. You will have more than enough for you and your family when you're generous.

"And my God will liberally supply (fill until full) your every need according to His riches in glory by Christ Jesus" (Philippians 4:19, AMP).

God Has Given You a Gift to Share

For as long as I can remember, I've awakened to my husband praying and reading his Bible in the early morning hours. It's incredible how his faithful study of the Word and his consistent relationship with Lord inspires me in my walk with the Lord. He's a wealth of knowledge and wisdom, and I can go to him for advice and answers any time of the day or night. But sometimes I might not like the wisdom he shares with me because it challenges me to do something that's totally out of my comfort zone.

I know it's hard to believe, but I do have a stubborn side to my personality. I've had a bad habit of looking at my limited abilities when I should be looking to God to supply me with everything I need. I don't always want to follow godly advice, but every time I do, God teaches me something new.

"To know wisdom and instruction; to perceive the words of understanding; to receive the instruction of wisdom, justice, and judgment, and equity; to give subtilty to the simple, to the young man knowledge and discretion. A wise man will hear and will increase learning; and a man of understanding shall attain unto wise counsels: to understand the proverb, and the interpretation; the words of the wise, and their dark sayings. The fear of the Lord is the beginning of knowledge: but fools despise wisdom and instruction" (Proverbs 1:2-7, KJV).

God will challenge you and me to be generous and share what we have in seemingly the most ridiculous of circumstances. He wants to see if we'll respond in faith to His Word, so He can bless us. He'll ask us to plant our little seed in the most unlikely seasons of our lives. God has continued to challenge me to do more than I think I can do and He wants to challenge you today to share the gifts and talents He's given to you!

"Give, and you'll receive. Your gift will return to you in full—pressed down, shaken together to make room for more, running over, and poured into your lap. The amount you give will determine the amount you get back" (Luke 6:38, NLT).

When our son, Jordan, graduated from high school twelve years ago, my husband and I were so excited to see him in his cap and gown, moving on to the next phase of his life. I was especially elated to be out of this season—raising children and helping with homework. A few short months after his graduation I was once again totally blindsided by my husband's proposal—He asked me to direct the children's ministry department at our church. This new opportunity, as he called it, was so far removed from where I wanted to go in this next stage of my life. I had visions of relaxing in a lounge chair on the beach, listening to the crashing waves and reading a good book.

Again, my husband had a totally different plan for my future. Evidently, he thought I was equipped and up for this new challenge. Let me explain: I was out of the children's ministry business—volunteering for the nursery, the three-and-four-year-old class, the junior high and high schoolers—that part of my life was over. Well, the next few days after that conversation, I cried and poured out my complaints to God. I said: "Why are you always asking me to do things that I don't know how to do? Why now and why me?"

Of course, one day soon after my husband's request, I was reading my Bible and I ran across this verse:

"God has given each of you a gift from his great variety of spiritual gifts. Use them well to serve one another. Do you have the gift of speaking? Speak as though God were speaking through you. Do you have the gift of helping others? Do it with all the energy and strength God supplies and everything you do will bring glory to God through Jesus Christ" (1 Peter 4:10, NLT).

What gifts has God given to you to share with others? God isn't asking you to be a Ph.D. before you can help someone else. He's asking you to share the gifts that He's given you. He will supply the energy and the strength that you need as you share your gifts.

I knew that God had given me gifts to share and He asked me a question, "Kathy, what have I put in your hand? I didn't ask you if you were qualified or even in the mood. I'm asking you to share what I've given you." I answered, "I'm good at supporting people, but I'm not qualified to direct the children's ministry. I don't have training in that arena and I feel weak."

I knew that God wanted me to support the hundreds of volunteers at our church and make sure they had everything they needed to prosper. He reminded me that even though I felt weak, I would be strong in Him. I could go to Him for guidance and strength every time I needed His help. He's not expecting you to give something you don't have, but He does want you to share what you have for the benefit others.

"There are different kinds of spiritual gifts, but the same Spirit as the source of them all. There are different kinds of service, but we serve the same Lord. God works in different ways, but it is the same God who does the work in all of us. A spiritual gift is given to each of us, so we can help each other. To one person the Spirit gives the ability to give wise advice, to another the same Spirit gives a message of special knowledge. The same Spirit gives great faith to another, and to someone else the one Spirit gives the gift of healing. He gives one person the power to perform miracles, and another the ability to prophesy. He gives someone else the ability to discern whether a message is from the Spirit of God or from another spirit. Still another person is given the ability to speak in unknown languages, while another is given the ability to interpret what is being said. It is the one and only Spirit who distributes all these gifts. He alone decides which gift each person should have" (I Corinthians 12:4-11, NLT).

The widow of Zarephath had no clue that God would use her ability to cook to sustain her household and keep Elijah alive. It wouldn't surprise me if she was shocked to see her jars of oil and flour bins miraculously refilled every time she shared them. She shared the little she had, and God multiplied it. It's very exciting to share God's gifts and see His miraculous provision for others.

IT'S TIME TO REFLECT

One of the most important Fall activities is getting some perspective. If the harvest has been small, it's time to reflect on what you can do differently next time. Rather than live in regret, confess your weakness and ask God to help you. Then think through what you're going to do differently next time, so you can gain a better harvest.

"Yet God has made everything beautiful for its own time. He has planted eternity in the human heart, but even so, people cannot see the whole scope of God's work from beginning to end" (Ecclesiastes 3:11, NLT).

Though we can't fully understand what God is doing in our season, we can trust that He does everything right on time. Reflect on how He's working in you through every season, even the disappointing ones. You never know what God can bring forth out of a hard season because He makes all things beautiful in His time.

What Season Are You In?

Today, I want you to reflect on seasons of your life and look for God's purpose in your "now." See yourself in the context of spiritual seasons in the different parts of your life. Where are you today?

- **In your finances?** If you're in the Spring, get your seed into the ground and expect a harvest. If you're in Winter, choose to dream again. Make some goals and be sure to bless your faithful God.

"Though the fig tree does not bud and there are no grapes on the vines... yet I will rejoice in the Lord, I will be joyful in God my Savior" (Habakkuk 3:17-18, NIV).

- **In your relationships?** This may be a Springtime for you–or it could be you're in a Winter, with Spring yet ahead. You may wish to be married, or you wish you hadn't, but trust Him and say with David:

"The Lord will work out his plans for my life–for your faithful love, O Lord, endures forever" (Psalm 138:8, NLT).

- **In your ministry?** For those in the hard, dry ministry season, it is tiring work, but don't forget that there will be a harvest that glorifies God. God is not mocked, and if you sow, God will bring the increase.

"Therefore, my beloved brethren, be steadfast, immovable, always abounding in the work of the Lord, knowing that your toil is not in vain in the Lord" (1 Corinthians 15:58, NASB).

- **In your walk with God?** You may feel a million miles away from God and in a spiritual Winter. God wills to bring you to the season of celebration and praise! You have been forgiven, and God will never abandon you. Walk out your faith in obedience and get ready for big things.

"But the seed planted in the good earth represents those who hear the Word, and embrace it, and produce a harvest beyond their wildest dreams" (Mark 4:20, MSG).

Remember: Fall is your time of fulfillment and joy because God has faithfully rewarded your trust in Him. You can't control your season, but you can believe God's promises right now.

Discussion Questions

Open Up: How did you first experience the glory of God?

Share Scriptures: Let different members/friends share a verse or idea from this chapter that impacted them personally. What does it mean for you?

Talk It Over: What fruit should you expect to produce in your Fall Season?

Pray Together: Pray for each other to be ready to see what God wants you to see in the Fall season.

    Prayer for the Fall Season:

Father God, thank you for bringing me through every season into a fruitful harvest. I celebrate today because I know you are opening my eyes to see beyond my natural circumstances and teaching me how to rejoice in my Fall season.

7
THIS IS YOUR BEST SEASON

When I think of the seasons I've been through I can clearly see how God's loving hand has directed me through every one of them. The message of understanding seasons is a powerful one because it teaches us God is in control and it's all been for our good. I can relate to the writer of Psalms when he says the Lord directs the steps of the godly and even though they stumble they will never fall, because the Lord holds them by the hand. (Psalm 37:23-24)

Throughout this chapter you will discover how God leads you through the dark nights of the soul, inspires you to get back up on your feet and helps you to move forward into the greatest season you've ever known. He's calling you and me to reach up into heavenly places and live in the abundant life He's planned for us.

COME WITH ME

"My beloved spoke and said to me, Arise... My beautiful one, come with me. See! the Winter is past the rains are over and gone. Flowers appear on the earth; the season of singing has come, and the voice of the turtledove is heard in our land" (Song of Solomon 2:10-12, NIV).

The Song of Solomon is a holy, spicy love story between a Shepherd King and a poor country girl. He serenades His lover with tender words, encourages her to arise from her Winter season and enter a season of singing. The romantic language in this poetic saga paints a picture of Jesus, your Shepard King, and how He longs to have a relationship with you. As you respond to His love, He'll bring healing to your heart and transform you into a strong, confident woman.

Jesus teaches us how a true shepherd lovingly tends, leads, guides, cherishes, feeds and protects His sheep. (John 10). In Psalm 23, King David says, The Lord is my Shepherd and I have everything I need—God leads me beside still waters, restores my soul, and comforts me in dark times. Your Shepherd King has supplied an amazing array of benefits for women just like you. He's inviting you to follow Him into beautiful places and take part in the good things He's created just for you.

"The Lord is my shepherd; I shall not want. He makes me to lie down in green pastures; He leads me beside still waters. He restores my soul; He leads me in the paths of righteousness for His name's sake. Yea, though I walk through the valley of the shadow of death, I will fear no evil; For you are with me; Your rod and Your staff, they comfort me. You prepare a table before me in the presence of my enemies; You anoint my head with oil; my cup runs over" (Psalm 23:1-5, NKJV).

Why does God say we're like sheep who need to be led into green pastures? I read an article the other day about the behavior of sheep and there's a good reason why the Bible says, *we all, like sheep, have gone astray, each of us has turned to our own way.* (Isaiah 53:6) Try not to be offended, but it's amazing how much we have in common with these animals. Sheep need to be led by their shepherd because they're inherently stupid and they get themselves into a lot of trouble without his guidance. Another way of saying that is: they're not too smart. They make every effort to do things on their own, but they really don't have the ability to do them all by themselves.

If I'm being honest with you, I don't want to be led by anyone, either. Most people who know me think that I'm submissive and sweet, but I'm really a sweet rebel. I have very strong opinions about where I want to go and when I want to go there. My mother told me one of the first words that came out of my mouth was "no."

But that stubborn nature can sometimes keep me from being led into the wonderful places God wants to take me.

Let me begin by sharing some of the things I've learned about sheep from their shepherds. Sheep are not very bright–they can't swim, but they repeatedly jump into streams, only to have to be rescued by their shepherd. Sheep will try to walk through barb-wired fences and get caught in them, only to go back and try again the next day. Sheep are very demanding and require an unlimited amount of grass, eating it all day and night. When they see their shepherd's fill their empty troughs, they run at him as though they're in a life and death situation. Sheep have a reputation of being stubborn—they have a long-standing habit of straying away from the rest of the flock and getting lost. (Luke 15:3)

They have no problem walking to the edge of a cliff, not realizing they could fall off at any moment. Sheep are very restless and don't sleep very long–they will be up in the middle of the night still eating grass in the wee hours of the morning, running across the field in no apparent direction. Shepherds will tell you, if sheep are going to lie down, they need to be free from fear, hunger and relieved from pests and parasites. They're very dependent on their shepherd's care and need constant supervision by him. Unless they have a shepherd guiding them they will probably not live very long.

After studying sheep, I could see myself as one of them, especially the stubborn ones who attempt to do things on their own only to get hurt in the process. I've learned a long time ago, if I'm going to live in green pastures, I need my Shepherd's tender care and guidance every day to get me there. We've all made decisions that have led us into situations that were harmful to us. Thank God, the Holy Spirit lives within us and teaches us everything we need to know. (1John 2:27)

Jesus is inviting you to follow Him into a place of unbelievable fulfillment and He wants to give you everything you need, but you'll have to allow Him to lead you to the still waters where He can restore your soul?

I'm so in Love with You

When the Shepherd King speaks to His beloved to arise into a season of singing, He's saying: What's happening in nature is a beautiful picture of what's taking place in your spiritual life—the Winter rains are in your past, Spring and the time for singing is here—this is your best season. Rise up and enter it with me.

There's nothing better than reading a great romance novel wherein the handsome prince saves the oppressed peasant girl from her tragic life. He provides her with a beautiful mansion and she inherits great wealth because of His love for her. I know some of those love stories are fictional, but they're inspirational and motivate me to reach higher into God's purpose for my life. I encourage you to read the picturesque love story in the Song of Solomon to get the full impact of God's never-ending love for you and how He wants to lead you into your best season ever.

Have you ever heard a little girl declare her love for her father and say she wants to marry him when she grows up? My granddaughter, Chloe, is three years old and I can see she's already a typical female who loves romance. She constantly tells my husband how much she loves him. What kind of grandmother would I be if I didn't tell stories about my grandchildren? She was playing hide and seek with my husband the other day in our home. They turn off all the lights in the house and use their flashlights to guide them. Chloe counts to ten and waits for my husband to hide somewhere in the house. Then she runs from room to room searching for him in each hiding place. When she finally finds him, she screams with delight and innocently declares her love, "Poppy, I'm so in love with you." You can believe, at that moment, he gives her whatever her little heart desires. She feels so loved when my husband gives her his undivided attention and says, "I'm in love with you, too, sweetheart."

It's not a cliché for me to say to you, "your best season is just ahead." Why? Seeking Jesus, and hearing his language of love for you, will transform you into the confident and secure woman you were created to be. When you understand how much He loves you, His love will cause you to arise and enter one of the best seasons of your life.

"For I know the thoughts that I think towards you, says the Lord, thoughts of peace and not of evil, to give you a future and I hope. Then you will call upon me and go and pray to Me and I will listen to you. And you will seek Me and find Me, when you search for Me with all your heart" (Jeremiah 29:11-13, NIV).

The Secret Places

Did you ever have a secret hiding place when you were younger? Was it a place you would go when you wanted to get away from the troubles of life? When I was a little girl I lived next to a big field with tall overgrown grass and fruit trees. My girlfriends and I built our own secret, cardboard fort where we knew we would could share our secrets with each other. This was not a place where everyone was invited, but only a few special friends knew about our secret hideaway.

"Oh, my dove, in the cleft of the rock, in the secret places of the cliff, let me see your face, let me hear your voice; for your voice is sweet, and your face is lovely" (Song of Solomon 2:14, NKJV).

God has a special hiding place and he's inviting you to join Him there. But He's not only asking you to visit Him occasionally, but He wants you to pack up your belongings and move in with Him.

Psalm 91:1 says: "Those who dwell in the secret place of the Most High God shall abide under the shadow of the Almighty." Dwelling under His shadow means we live directly under God's protection and we get to spend time with Him any time we need to be assured of His love.

Even Jesus found quiet places to go when He needed strength and guidance from His Father. He modeled the importance of connecting with God to His disciples. Jesus was one of the busiest people that ever lived on earth and He traveled from place to place—performing miracles and feeding thousands of people, but He chose to go to a secluded spot to hear from His Father. There were days that were so full of His Father's work, He didn't have time to eat. (Mark 1:35) Even Jesus, the Son of God, needed to get refreshed and refilled from time to time.

There are so many benefits for women who live in the secret place with God. It's so important for you to plan a time in your day when you can meet with Him. Psalms 91 says because you have made the Lord your dwelling place, wonderful things will happen for you. Here are the promises you can expect God to fulfill when you set your affections on Him.

- Find rest in His fortress
- He will save you from snares and deadly diseases
- Cover you with his feathers and find refuge
- Shield you with His faithfulness
- You will not fear night terrors or flying arrows
- You will not fear pestilence in the night
- You will not fear plagues in the midday
- Thousands falling all around you will not come near you
- You will watch the wicked being punished
- No harm will overtake you, no disaster will come near your house

- Angels will guard you in all your ways and lift you up in their hands
- You will tread on lions and cobras
- He will rescue you and protect you when you acknowledge Him
- When you call, He will answer you
- He will be with you in trouble, deliver you and honor you
- You will be satisfied with long life and He will show you His salvation

I know women are pulled into a hundred different directions every day with so many responsibilities—taking care of our families—elderly parents and sick children, driving to and from work, grocery shopping, cooking meals, managing business affairs and cleaning our homes; but if we'll make God a priority in our day, we'll not be sorry we did.

Jesus said you'll be openly rewarded when you talk to God in the secret place.

"But when you pray, go into your room, and when you have shut the door, pray to your Father who is in the secret place; and your Father who sees in secret will reward you openly" (Matthew 6:6, NJKV).

From Glory to Glory He's Changing Me

"Then Moses said, 'Now show me your glory.' And the LORD said, 'I will cause all my goodness to pass in front of you, and I will proclaim my name, the LORD, in your presence. I will have mercy on whom I will have mercy, and I will have compassion on whom I will have compassion. But,' he said, 'you cannot see my face, for no one may see me and live.' Then the LORD said, 'There is a place near me where you may stand on a rock. When my glory passes by, I will put you in a cleft in the rock and cover you with my hand until I have passed by. Then I will remove my hand and you will see my back; but my face must not be seen'" (Exodus 33:18-23, NIV).

I love this interaction between God and Moses when God puts Moses in a safe place to reveal His goodness, mercy, and compassion to Him. He tells him to stand on a rock and then puts him in a hiding place to share who He is with Moses.

The Bible says when you and I get real with God we will see His glory. When we invite His presence into those secret places of our hearts, that's when He begins to change us little by little. The more we let Him into the secret places of our hearts, the Holy Spirit touches us with God's goodness and compassion. As you and I get closer to our Shepherd King we are changed into His likeness.

"And we all, with unveiled face, beholding the glory of the Lord, are being transformed into the same image from one degree of glory to another. For this comes from the Lord who is the Spirit" (2 Corinthians 3:18, ESV).

For example, when Jesus called his disciples to follow Him, can you imagine what it was like for them to be with Jesus day and night? They heard first-hand his messages and had all the parables explained to them afterward. They saw the sick healed and dead people raised from their graves.

When Jesus took Peter, John, and James with him to pray, Luke 9 tells the story of what happened on the Mount of Transfiguration. As Jesus was praying, His appearance became a dazzling white. Moses and Elijah appeared and talked to Jesus. Peter said, "Master, it's wonderful for us to be here! Let's build tabernacles here." In other words, "This is the best. Let's stay here and enjoy the glory."

What was that all about? Peter wanted to stay on the mountaintop and bask in the Lord's glory. But the Bible tells us that Peter didn't know what he was saying. Here's what Peter needed to know: if they stayed on the glorious mountain, they would have missed all the other experiences Jesus had prepared for their lives.

"The way of the righteous is like the first gleam of dawn, which shines ever brighter until the full light of day. The way of the righteous is like the first gleam of dawn, which shines ever brighter until the full light of day" (Proverbs 4:18, NLT).

From glory to glory He's changing me, changing me, changing me. His likeness and image to perfect in me, the love that God's shown to the world. For he's changing, changing me, from earthly things to the heavenly. His likeness and image to perfect in me, the love that God's shown to the world. These are the words to one of the songs that my church sang in the early seventies and every time I sang it, I believed that God was changing me to be like Him.

What does it mean when God's glory touches our lives? His glory affects our innermost being and His goodness and compassion change us. The Holy Spirit overshadows us and enables us to love others, to feel compassion for the grieving and accomplish great things for Him. We start to look and act like Jesus. We take on His mannerisms and we do what He did when He was here on earth. Our loved ones and friends begin to ask us questions like, "What's different about you?" People will say things like, "Whatever you have, I want it."

You and I are called to follow Jesus as His disciples and we'll have many incredible moments in that process. When we have a mountaintop experience and get a glimpse of His glory we may ask to stay there. But the Lord is calling us to arise and follow Him into more. Remember, in Christ, your best season is just ahead!

YOU ARE WITH ME

Many years ago, I was only a teenager—barely saved and a baby Christian—but I had recently given my life to Jesus and encountered the glory of God in a major way. I wanted to tell my friends and family what Jesus did for me. I wanted to see people healed from their hurts. I was always talking to my girlfriends about Jesus.

One day one of them called me crying with terrible news about her little brother. She said he was riding his friend's motorcycle and crashed it into a parked car on her street. Her brother, who had just turned sixteen, was rushed to the hospital emergency room. She asked if I would come to the hospital because he was in critical condition and hanging onto his life by breathing machines.

When I arrived at the hospital, there were about twenty people in the waiting room—they all had sad, swollen faces from crying. I'm not usually a person who takes charge, but a boldness came over me and I instructed everyone to stand and hold hands. To my amazement, everyone in the room followed my lead. They all stood and held each other's hands because they were desperate to feel God's comfort during this dark moment. Sad to say, my friend's brother didn't live to see his eighteenth birthday, but the entire family told me after we prayed, they felt the sweet, calming presence of God envelop them. They knew that God was with them as they walked through this dark valley together.

"The Lord is my shepherd; I shall not want... Yea, though I walk through the valley of the shadow of death, I will fear no evil; For you are with me; Your rod and Your staff they comfort me" (Psalm 23:1, 4, NKJV).

She Believed God was with Her Every Step of the Way

I was so happy when Sharon came into my life because that meant I wasn't going to have to be my husband's Administrative Assistant any longer. You might be thinking, "how could a pastor's wife say such an awful thing—don't you love working with your husband?"

When my husband and I returned from the mission field in 1988, we resumed working for our church and we were both given new positions on the staff. He was asked to be the Senior Associate Pastor and I was hired as his assistant. This was new territory for me and I learned quickly it's not as easy as it looks to be a pastor's wife or his assistant.

The challenging part of my job was saying 'no' to people who called our office and wanted to meet with my husband on a moment's notice. I didn't want our congregation to see me as the person who said, "No, he's not available right now—you'll have to make an appointment to see him." They didn't understand that he wasn't always available at the very moment they wanted to talk to him. Sometimes they would get upset and let me know they weren't too happy with me. I wanted our church family to see me as the "sweet pastor's wife" who's always available to heal their hurts, not say 'no' to them. Of course, I was more than willing to support my husband as his assistant, but I was thrilled when Sharon became part of our team. She was an experienced Executive Administrative Assistant. She was so good at her job and didn't have a problem saying "no" in the nicest possible way. Smile.

As I got to know Sharon, I realized that she was a multi-talented woman who loved the Lord and had a servant's heart. She and her husband, Dennis, opened their home for small group Bible studies and loved the people that were in their group. Not only was she good at assisting my husband, but she always looked very sharp and professional—perfectly styled hair and impeccable makeup.

She never gave me the impression that she had been through a long list of difficult and heartbreaking circumstances prior to working at the church. The longer we worked together, I began to understand the trials Sharon went through in her childhood and later in her adult life.

Sharon told me she had vivid childhood memories of her parents fighting and being spanked with wooden hangers until they broke. Her father's frequent drinking caused yelling and abusive behavior in her home. He eventually moved out and her mother told her the reason he left them was because he didn't love them anymore. By the time she was nine years old she became responsible to take care of her little sister, was assigned household chores like preparing dinner for the family. Her mother remarried by the time Sharon entered junior high school and she felt displaced and unloved by her new stepfather.

Sharon's first marriage was a loveless one, filled with criticism and rejection by her husband. This led to feelings of insecurity and a deep desire to be noticed by other men. When her married boss told her how beautiful she was—his attention was too hard to resist, and she was drawn to him by his kind words. She agreed to meet with him at a nearby hotel. As you can imagine, one thing led to another and Sharon slept with him.

Finally, she felt loved and wanted by a man—only he was a married man with children of his own. They fell more in love and discovered she was pregnant a few months later with her first son. She wondered how she was going to explain this to her mother-in-law, who knew she and her husband hadn't slept together for years. So, she lied to her and told her they had slept together once and that's how she became pregnant.

Jeffrey Mark was born on April 3, 1967, after thirty hours of labor. She was thrilled to be a mother, but she had since cut off her adulteress relationship with her boss. Sharon was determined to be a great mother and raise her baby boy in a good family—so she endeavored to make her faulty marriage work. Jeffrey was the center of her world and she threw herself into her new role as mommy. One day as she was laying him down in his crib she had a premonition and heard an inaudible voice say, "he will not live past the age of two." Those words were like getting hit by a lightning bolt, but she ignored the voice of doom. She tried to work things out with her first husband, but that relationship kept twirling on a downward spiral.

She resumed her extramarital affair with her son's father and they met as often as possible to dote on their child. They decided it would be best to divorce their spouses and move in together to start their new lives. Never in a million years had Sharon dreamed she would be "the other woman." Her two-year-old son was introduced to his new grandparents, followed by expressions of joy and tender tears. But her stepfather and mother were not as easily on board with Sharon's lifestyle and were very angry with her.

Jeffrey was the typical toddler who loved to climb, suck his thumb and tried to get into everything he could get his hands on. One day when Sharon was running her errands, she came back home with a car full of groceries. As she turned to take Jeffrey out of his car seat, he said, "Jeffy, do it byself!" Sharon headed to the front door, assuming he was following her, she heard the phone ringing and went into the house to answer it. She turned to see Jeffrey wasn't in the house. When she went outside to look for him, she heard a man yelling, "help, help!" Her car had rolled into the driveway and halfway out into the street—the man was holding the car to keep it from rolling backward. Jeffrey was under the car and the front wheel was on his head.

Saturday, November 15, 1969, Sharon's world was turned upside down because her little boy, Jeffrey, was run over by her car and died that day. She remembers telling the police officer the devastating details of what happened that day. By the time she was finished telling him what happened, he too was in tears sharing her pain. It was by the grace of God that she survived this ordeal, but words are not sufficient to describe the agony of losing her baby boy. Sharon spent many days alone with no one to talk to, focusing on her guilt and overwhelming sadness. She felt responsible for her son's death and felt like a complete failure. She truly believed she was being punished for conceiving her child in an adulterous affair.

Sharon and her boss were married in January of 1970 and they were blessed with two more beautiful children: a precious baby girl and a little boy.

Looking back over her terrible Winter season she believes God was with her every step of the way. She began to search for answers and was desperate to find the comfort that she needed to be completely healed from the guilt and shame she felt every day. She began to delve into all sorts of occult practices, astrological chart readings, numerology and getting her palm read. These are all activities that she later learned God calls abominations in Deuteronomy 18:9-14.

Although it would seem her little family should have been happy, they were not. Her second marriage did not last very long, and her husband moved on to greener pastures. They were divorced by the time their children were three and eighteen months old. She was back to being alone and vulnerable—another man had stopped loving her. She began to ask herself questions about her life: Why was life going so badly and what was so wrong with her that she kept ending up alone?

Mommy, Who's Jesus?

By the time Sharon's children were in the first and second grade she was in her third unhappy marriage. In June 1976, seven years after Jeff died, Sharon had not forgiven God for taking her son. But one day her daughter, who was five at the time, came home from playing with a friend. She asked her, "mommy, who's Jesus?"

Sharon felt the need to go to church and investigate the answer for her daughter. Their little family began attending a Christian church together. The people in this church seemed happy and excited about life and her children loved going there. Sharon heard a message one Sunday about God being her Heavenly Father, how He loved her and wanted to take care of her.

Sharon said—

I understood that God has a distinct purpose for each one of us, and by choosing to do things his way, I would be able to accomplish that special thing that he created me to do. So far, my being in control of my life hasn't been too successful. And really, what did I have to lose? From my outward appearance, people thought I had it all altogether, never knowing what anguish, unrest, and guilt still languished on the inside of me like a stagnant pond. I decided I needed this relationship with God and I knew it would take a great amount of faith to follow through. In July 1976, I accepted Jesus as my personal savior. It was a most amazing experience; I was truly changed on the inside. I felt like the weight of the world had been lifted from my shoulders; an unexplainable happiness just bubbled up on the inside of me.

This was Sharon's first encounter with God's glory and His goodness. She accepted His forgiveness of her many sins that day and wanted to stay in His unbelievable presence, but God had so much more for her to understand about His love for her.

She tells the incredible story of her life in her book, *From Tragedy to Triumph.* Her life is a testament of how God's mercy and power can restore a broken life.

"Yet God has made everything beautiful for its own time. He has planted eternity in the human heart, but even so, people cannot see the whole scope of God's work from beginning to end" (Ecclesiastes 3:11, NIV).

RISE UP INTO YOUR BEST SEASON

Perhaps you're reading this chapter and can relate to some of Sharon's painful past experiences. You might be struggling to believe that you can rise into your best season because you've been reliving and rehearsing those dark moments of your past. Sharon experienced those dark valleys, too, but she had to make a conscious decision to follow the Lord and believe that He was leading her out of darkness into His beautiful light.

Look at the promise He's made to you in John 8:12. You can rise to your best season when you choose to follow Him into His light.

"If you follow me, you won't have to walk in darkness, because you will have the light that leads you" (John 8:12, NIV).

He Leads Me Beside Still Waters

God is very aware of your mistakes and failures and that's why He sent the Good Shepherd to lead you beside still waters and bring restoration to your soul. If you and I are going to experience everything He has promised us in Psalm 23—the green pastures, the still waters and a place at His table, we'll have to let go of the tight grip we have on our past and start believing the good things He has prepared for us right now. Let God lead you into the place where His glory, goodness, and compassion live.

Sharon was a product of the cruel words that were spoken to her by her parents when they sat her down to tell her they were getting a divorce. She was sent the message from her mother that her father didn't love her. Whether it was our parents sitting us down to tell us they were getting a divorce, or we were sent other messages about our worth when someone abandoned us—these hurtful things can greatly impact our lives.

Unfortunately, many women just stay stuck in the hurtful experiences of their past. They believe the condemning words that were spoken to them by their loved ones. They constantly look back in the rearview mirror and rehearse old hurts over and over in their minds. It's hard for them to believe that they will arise to everything God has provided for their future. One of the keys to arising into our best season is letting go of our past.

"One thing I do, forgetting those things which are behind and reaching forward to those things which are ahead. I press toward the goal for the prize of the upward call of God in Christ Jesus" (Philippians 3:13-14, NKJV).

He Restores My Soul

I want you to look at Psalm 23 and think about all your needs being met by the Good Shepherd. Let Him lead you to still waters and allow Him to completely restore your soul. Your soul is the place where your mind (your thought life), your will (your decisions), and your emotions (your feelings) are stored.

God wants to bring rest to your every part of your soul, so you can relax in His presence and release you from emotional turmoil. He wants to meet all your needs and help you understand you're secure when you spend time with Him.

There's a process of restoration that God wants to take you through, and He will supply you with an abundance of His grace to help you into your new season. The grace of God is packed full of His kindness, favor, mercy, beauty, and love.

"For if by the one man's offense death reigned through the one, much more those who receive abundance of grace and of the gift of righteousness will reign in life through one man, Jesus Christ" (Romans 5:17, NJKV).

The New Testament talks about renewing your mind with the Word of God and how it brings life and peace to your thought processes. God will restore your soul as you rest by His still waters. He will guide and help you make right decisions as you spend time with Him in the secret place.

Jesus is knocking on the door of your heart–the book of Revelation says so...He's asking if He can come into the secret places of your life that need to be healed. Will you let Him into your heart and allow Him to restore your soul?

"Behold, I stand at the door and knock. If anyone hears My voice and opens the door, I will come in to him and dine with him, and he with Me" (Revelation 3:20, NKJV).

You're Accepted in the Beloved

As we read the love story in *The Song of Solomon*, we hear the loving words the Shepherd-King lavishes on His beloved. You and I are His beloved and we're one hundred percent accepted by Jesus. I want you to take a moment and think about the words that Jesus is speaking to you today and decide that you're going to listen to His voice.

"Having predestined us to adoption as sons by Jesus Christ Himself, according to the good pleasure of his will, to the praise of the glory of his grace, by which He made us accepted in the Beloved" (Ephesians 1:5-6, NKJV).

He Prepares a Table for Me

"You prepare a table before me in the presence of my enemies..." (Psalm 23:5a, NIV).

A few days ago, I was having a lovely middle eastern meal with my husband on our day off. We sat down and ordered the most delicious skewered chicken and steak kabobs, roasted to perfection– with a side of creamy hummus, garnished with paprika and warm rice. We looked across the table into each other's eyes and I began to speak. You would think that I would take advantage of being in the presence of this handsome man that I have known for the last forty-three years. But that's not what happened, I started our conversation with some drama that was happening in our church. I saw a look of sadness on my husband's face and he lovingly held my hands and said, "I don't want to talk about problems right now, let's enjoy our day and talk about happy things."

This is a picture of what we often do to God when He's trying to get us to see the wonderful table He's prepared for our lives. We bring up all the ugly things that have happened in our lives during the most amazing life He's planned for us.

My husband was correct to steer me in the right direction. We were in the middle of celebrating this scrumptious meal—this was my opportunity to once again gaze into his golden, brown eyes and enjoy our beautiful day. I had to remember what God says in the book of Psalms, He has prepared a beautiful table for me.

God has prepared a beautiful place setting with your name on it. He wants to give you an amazing picture of what your life can be— you're seated right next to Him where you belong.

This is your best season ever—it's time for you to enjoy the bountiful harvest He has prepared for you. Psalms 23 ends with God's goodness and mercy following you all the days of your life. He has made every spiritual blessing available to you.

"Praise be to the God and father of our Lord Jesus Christ, who has blessed us and the heavenly realms with every spiritual blessing in Christ. For he chose us in him before the creation of the world to be holy and blameless in his site. In love, he predestined us for adoption to Sonship through Jesus Christ, in accordance with his pleasure and will—what he has freely given us and the one he loves" (Ephesians 1:3-6, NIV).

You're Seated in Heavenly Places

I can't end this book without sharing the inspirational story of a woman who knew who she was in Christ. She believed that she was seated in heavenly places with Him. She knew the amazing benefits she had because she was a true follower of Jesus. She was born into a family who taught her Scriptures like Psalm 23:5-6: "*You prepare a table before me in the presence of my enemies; You anoint my head with oil; My cup runs over. Surely goodness and mercy shall follow me all the days of my life; And I will dwell in the house of the Lord forever.*" Her parents prayed with her every day before she went to pick cotton in the cotton fields.

Rosa Parks was awarded the Congressional Gold Medal, one of the highest honors given to a civilian, because she refused to give up her bus seat to a white man. Why was she able to be so determined to stay in her seat? Her confidence came from knowing where she was really seated: in heavenly places with Jesus and she was not going to give up her place for anyone.

Her life story speaks to thousands of women to stay seated in their rightful place, and to be careful to listen to Jesus. Don't let society, your broken family, or even a man, remove you from your rightful place with God. It's time for you to rise to your best season and sit in heavenly places where you belong.

"...made us alive with Christ, even when we were dead in our trespasses. It is by grace you have been saved! And God raised us up with Christ and seated us with him and heavenly realms in Christ Jesus" (Ephesians 2:6, BSB).

Every day you can choose to take your place at His bountiful table and eat every delicious dish He's prepared for you.

Every 24 hours there's a new day. Every seven days there's a new week. Every thirty days there's a new month. Every twelve months there's a new year. When you have Christ, you're constantly empowered to arise and follow Him. The beautiful thing about following Jesus is… you never have to go one minute without his grace and his love guiding you. He's calling you to follow Him into your best season and believe that His plans are to prosper you and not harm you. Believe that His plans are full of hope and He will give you an amazing future. (Jeremiah 29:11)

Because of Christ, your best season is yet ahead. Let go of the past, choose God's purpose in your present, and rise by faith into your future. This is your best season. Praise God!

Discussion Questions

Open Up: How did you first experience the love of God?

Share Scriptures: Let different members/friends share a verse or idea from this chapter that impacted them personally. What does it mean for you?

Talk It Over: What are some ways you can let the Good Shepherd guide you?

Pray Together: Pray for each other to be ready to listen to God's voice.

Prayer for your Best Season:

Father God, thank you for bringing me to the best season of my life. You're calling me to rise to the bountiful table you've prepared for me. I choose to follow you with all my heart. I accept your grace and forgiveness by faith, and I praise you for the awesome season ahead. Amen!

Contact the Author

Kathy Cannistraci

GateWay City Church
5883 Eden Park Place
San Jose, CA 95138

Kathy.Cannistraci@GateWayCityChurch.org

www.ingramcontent.com/pod-product-compliance
Lightning Source LLC
Chambersburg PA
CBHW052047070526
44584CB00017B/2083